Controversies in Sociology
edited by
Professor T. B. Bottomore and
Professor M. J. Mulkay

22
Choice, Rationality, and Social Theory

Controversies in Sociology

Choice, Rationality, and Social Theory

BARRY HINDESS

Australian National University

London
UNWIN HYMAN
Boston   Sydney   Wellington

Published by the Academic Division of
Unwin Hyman Ltd
15/17 Broadwick Street, London W1V 1FP, UK

Unwin Hyman, Inc,
8 Winchester Place, Winchester, Mass. 01890, USA

Allen & Unwin (Australia) Ltd,
8 Napier Street, North Sydney, NSW 2060, Australia

Allen & Unwin (New Zealand) Ltd in association with
the Port Nicholson Press Ltd,
60 Cambridge Terrace, Wellington, New Zealand

First published in 1988

British Library Cataloguing in Publication Data

Hindess, Barry
    Choice, rationality and social theory.
    (Controversies in sociology; 22).
    1. Social sciences. Concepts : Rationality –
    Philosophical perspectives
    I. Title   II. Series
    300'.1

ISBN   0-04-301306-6

Library of Congress Cataloging-in-Publication Data

Hindess, Barry.
    Choice, rationality and social theory.
    (Controversies in sociology ; 22)
    Bibliography: p.
    Includes index.
    1. Social choice. 2. Choice (Psychology)
    I. Title. II. Series.
HB846.8.H56   1988   302'.13   88–10698
ISBN 0-04-301306-6 (alk. paper)

Typeset in 10 on 12 point Times
and printed in Great Britain by
Billing and Sons, London and Worcester

Contents

Acknowledgements

Many people have helped in the production of this book, through their encouragement, critical discussion and disagreement and through reading and commenting on the manuscript. I am particularly grateful to Tom Bottomore, Frank Cunningham, Stephen Gaukroger, Paul Hirst, Ann Jungmann, Elizabeth Kingdom, Philip Pettit and Gary Wickham.

1
Introduction

The terms 'choice' and 'rationality' are used in many different ways in the social sciences, but one of the most influential contemporary usages is to identify rationality with behaviour that maximizes the satisfaction of preferences. The rational choice approach proposes to analyse human behaviour on the assumption that actors are rational in just that sense. Much of social life is then to be explained as the outcome of the rational choices of individual actors. The argument of this book is directed against that and related explanatory usages of the notion of individual rationality. There are, of course, other influential conceptions of rationality (for example, in critical theory) but they are not my concern here.

Models of maximizing behaviour are widely used in economics, and rational choice analysis can be understood as extending that economic approach to other areas of human behaviour. It is in this spirit that Gary Becker informs us that the economic approach

> is applicable to all human behaviour, be it behaviour involving money prices or imputed shadow prices, repeated or infrequent decisions, large or minor decisions, emotional or mechanical ends, rich or poor persons, men or women, adults or children, brilliant or stupid persons, businessmen or politicians, teachers or students. (Becker, 1976, p. 8)

Becker goes on to suggest that too many social scientists are tempted to hide their own lack of understanding of their subjects' behaviour behind allegations of 'ignorance and irrationality, values and their frequent and unexplained shifts, custom and tradition, the compliance somehow induced by social norms, or the ego and the id' (ibid., p. 13). Here those of us who fail to adopt the economic approach are accused of a kind of intellectual deceit, hiding our own ignorance behind talk of the irrationality of others. Becker is far from being alone in claiming the moral high ground for his own theoretical assumptions and condemning those who disagree, and not all who do so favour his economic approach[1] – but it is a style of argument that deserves little consideration.

Becker's argument on this point represents the weakest case for rational choice analysis, but there are more serious arguments to be considered. Adherents of rational choice analysis have claimed that it is rigorous, capable of great technical sophistication and able to generate powerful explanations across a wide range of situations on the basis of a few, relatively simple theoretical assumptions.[2] It also appears to take more seriously than sociological functionalism or structuralism the point that actors do indeed make decisions and act on them. It insists that actors are not mere creatures of their position in some overarching societal totality. No one, of course, would be so foolish as to maintain that action is always rational. The claim of rational choice analysis is not so much that the assumption of rationality is descriptively accurate but rather that it performs an important heuristic function: it is a useful simplification and it provides the means of identifying the place of non-rational elements in human behaviour.

On this view, non-rational elements may be introduced in our analyses only when explanation in rational terms has clearly failed. Jon Elster, for example, clearly recognizes that action is not always rational and that there are problems with the identification of rationality with maximizing behaviour. He nevertheless insists that 'explanation in terms of optimization remains the paradigm case of intentional explanation in the social sciences outside psychology' (Elster, 1983a, p. 75). All other cases of intentional explanation are then to be understood as involving specific departures from the paradigmatic norm.

This book is a critical discussion of some of the more serious claims of rational choice analysis. The clarity and technical sophistication of much rational choice analysis seem to me undeniable, and I do not dispute its claim to a certain kind of rigour. Unfortunately, those positive features of rational choice analysis depend on the adoption of a number of highly questionable assumptions about actors and about their rationality. Those assumptions are the target of my critical discussion. I argue that the theoretical parsimony and explanatory power of rational choice analysis are bought at far too high a theoretical cost, and I dispute both the assumption of actors' rationality and the paradigmatic status assigned to it.

It is important to be clear what is at stake in this last point. It would not be difficult to find instances of behaviour that seem far from rational, or areas of social life where the assumptions of the economic approach appear not to be appropriate. Hardin, for example, suggests that those assumptions yield 'a notoriously poor explanation of voting behaviour' (Hardin, 1982, p. 11) and Barry (1978) makes a similar point for political participation in general. Or again, sympathetic critics like Sen and Elster, and others who are not so sympathetic, have argued for a more complex view of actors' rationality than is normally provided in rational choice models.

Now, such points may dispose of Becker's more extravagant assertions but in themselves they do little damage to the more serious claims of rational choice analysis. These treat the assumption of rationality as a simplifying assumption, on the grounds that while it is not always realistic it does provide a paradigm for the analysis of other cases. In effect, we start from the assumption of rationality and consider other possibilities only when explanation in rational terms has clearly failed. The result of this manoeuvre is that criticism based on cases of non-rational behaviour or on a more sophisticated notion of actors' rationality can often be deflected without much difficulty. Of course, the argument goes, people are not always rational, but the assumption of rationality allows us to identify cases where other elements affect their behaviour. Of course, people are not always narrowly self-interested, but the assumption that they are allows us to identify the role of other motivations in their behaviour.

The point of claiming paradigmatic status for the model of optimizing behaviour is not then to deny the existence of other forms of behaviour. On the contrary, it recognizes cases where the assumption of actors' rationality does not apply and identifies their theoretical location – precisely as specific complications of or departures from the paradigmatic norm.[3] I argue that important questions of the forms of thought employed by actors and the social conditions on which they depend are obscured by the paradigm of optimizing behaviour.

The chapter following this short introduction provides a preliminary sketch of the basic structure of rational choice models and the variety of their applications, taking examples from a number of areas – discussions of government taxation and spending policies, explanations of economic growth and decline, and attempts to elaborate a rational choice Marxism. Many authors claim to draw political conclusions from their abstract analyses. In *The Rise and Decline of Nations*, to take just one example, Olson concludes that 'the best macro-economic policy is a good microeconomic policy. There is no substitute for a more open and competitive environment' (Olson, 1982, p. 233). Not all supporters of the rational choice approach would agree with Olson on this point. Nevertheless, his attempt to draw political conclusions from abstract analyses of the behaviour of rational actors raises important questions of what we should look for in discussions of social phenomena. I return to that issue in the concluding chapter.

Chapter 3 continues this preliminary discussion by examining the distinctive model of the actor employed in the rational choice approach. First, actors are assumed to act rationally in terms of a relatively stable set of beliefs and desires. Secondly, it is often supposed that they are narrowly self-interested. We shall see that this second assumption can be relaxed without serious damage to the rational choice approach. Finally, there is an explicit methodological individualism which presents the structural features of social life as if they were reducible to the actions of rational individuals and their (often unintended) consequences. I agree that actors' decisions should not be seen as effects of their positions in some overarching social structure, but it does not follow that social life is therefore reducible to the actions of individuals. Against that reductionism I argue in later chapters that actors' decisions and actions depend on conditions that are external to the actor concerned.

These two chapters prepare the ground for the critical argument that follows. The model of the actor employed in rational choice analysis involves specific refinements of a model that is widely used in philosophy and the social sciences. In this more general model, actors are assumed to be human individuals and their actions are supposed to follow from their beliefs, desires and other states of mind. In effect, the actor carries a portfolio of beliefs and desires around from one situation to another. Given the situation of action, the actor selects from its portfolio those elements that seem relevant and uses them to decide on a course of action. I call this the portfolio model of the actor. Rational choice analysis modifies the portfolio model in two important respects. First, it treats the actor's desires as exhibiting a utilitarian structure so that an optimal outcome can normally be defined in most situations confronting the actor. Secondly, it assigns a paradigmatic status to the assumption of rationality. I argue against the rational choice model both by questioning its refinements of the more general portfolio model and by disputing the portfolio model itself.

Chapter 4 discusses models of the actor. I begin by presenting an abstract concept of actor as locus of decision and action. Actors do things as a result of their decisions, and we call those things actions. Actors' decisions play an important part in the explanation of their actions. Actors may also do things that are not the result of any decision, and they must be explained in some other way. Now, the portfolio model builds far more into its concept of actor than is provided in the minimal concept presented here. First, it assumes that actors are human individuals. I argue on the contrary that there are important actors in the modern world other than human individuals. Capitalist enterprises, state agencies and political parties are all actors in the minimal sense that they have means of reaching decisions and of acting on some of them. Any analysis of modern societies that treats human individuals as the only effective actors must be regarded as seriously incomplete.

Secondly, the portfolio model treats action as a function of belief and desire. Intentional analysis then requires that we work back to actors' beliefs and desires by constructing an interpretation of their behaviour, including, of course, what they say. Disputes over rationality have played an important part in discussion of what is involved in understanding the behaviour of others and especially of other cultures.[4] Davidson and other philosophers have presented powerful arguments to the effect that the process of constructing an account of actors' beliefs and desires from observation of their behaviour in various contexts requires us to presume a fair degree of rationality and consistency in their behaviour. The assumption of rationality and consistency, which Davidson calls the principle of charity, would then be an essential part of any attempt to understand the behaviour of others. No discussion of the place of rationality in the analysis of human behaviour can afford to ignore these arguments.

Chapters 4 and 5 pay particular attention to the work of Donald Davidson, who has provided one of the clearest philosophical investigations of the character of intentional explanation. Chapter 4 examines the portfolio model and its assumption of an holistic rationality in detail. The final section contrasts the treatments of rationality in rational choice analysis and the more general portfolio model. The argument that interpretation of the behaviour of others requires a presumption of rationality does not entail the paradigmatic status which rational choice analysis claims for what it describes as rationality.

Chapter 5 questions the portfolio model itself by disputing Davidson's argument that intentional analysis must presuppose an holistic rationality. The problem with the treatment of action as resulting from belief and desire is that it says nothing about those processes of deliberation that sometimes play an important part in actors' decisions. More precisely, it takes the rationality of those processes for granted by treating them as transparent intermediaries between belief and desire on the one hand and the action that results from them on the other. Once some definite process of deliberation is admitted as an element in the actor's decision then that process and the techniques and forms of thought employed within it must be regarded as objects of investigation.

I consider two influential ways in which the rationality of actors' deliberations has been brought into question. One is Simon's concept of satisficing or bounded rationality, and the other is the claim that there are distinct 'rationalities' or styles of reasoning. The latter has to be treated with some care. A common way of looking at different ways of thinking is in terms of a distinction between conceptual schemes and reality: different schemes produce different perceptions of reality.[5] Davidson has shown that the conceptual relativism involved here cannot be sustained. But there is another relativism concerning distinct styles of reasoning that does not fall under Davidson's critique. This has devastating consequences for the assumption of an holistic rationality. First, if specialized techniques may be employed in actors' deliberations then the problem for intentional analysis is to identify those techniques and to investigate the conditions on which their usage depends, not to take their rationality for granted. Secondly, there is no reason to suppose that the specialized techniques employed by actors in different areas of their activity will be consistent with each other. There is no reason, in other words, to suppose that actors will exhibit an holistic rationality. The final section of the chapter shows that these arguments undermine the characterization of action in terms of a more or less stable portfolio of beliefs and desires.

The final chapter considers the implications of these arguments, both for rational choice analysis and for the portfolio model generally. Human individuals and social actors use conceptual and other tools in their deliberations. Societies will differ in the range and variety of conceptual tools that are available to their members. In any given society the use of some tools will be commonplace, and the use of others (the poison oracle, cost-benefit analysis, geomancy) will be relatively specialized. The concerns and objectives that motivate actors and the results of their deliberations will depend on the techniques and forms of thought they are able to employ. The problem with the portfolio model is not so much that it denies the place of deliberation in actors' decisions, but rather that it treats deliberation as if it were transparently rational and therefore of little explanatory significance. Rational choice analysis does the same, with a more restrictive notion of rationality. I argue on the contrary that the tools used by actors in their deliberations, their connections with other tools, and the ways in which they depend on social conditions are legitimate and important areas of investigation.

The concluding section returns to the claims of rational choice analysis to theoretical parsimony and explanatory power. I argue that many of the apparently powerful results of rational choice analysis depend on an implicit structural determination of the forms of thought employed by actors. The problem here is simply stated: the assumption of actors' rationality tells us that there will be a certain consistency in their behaviour, but it tells us nothing of the substance of their concerns. The explanation of social conditions and structural features of social life as resulting from the rational actions of large numbers of individuals therefore requires some further assumption regarding the social distribution of actors' concerns and objectives. The most common assumption is that what is to count as rational action for some particular actor is a function of that actor's membership of one of the social categories recognized by the rational choice model in question; political leaders, say, behave as they do because they are political leaders and because they are rational. Here an important part of actors' concerns is determined by the social conditions in which they find themselves. I argue on the contrary that actors' concerns and objectives depend in part on the techniques and forms of thought they are in a position to employ. While there are always connections between actors' social location and the forms of thought they employ in deciding on courses of action, there is no simple correspondence between them.

As for theoretical parsimony, rational choice analysis abstracts from the forms of thought employed by actors in their deliberations to produce an account of what hypothetical rational actors would do in their place. There are two important issues to be considered here. First, it is doubtful if any worthwhile political conclusions can be drawn from an analysis that deliberately abstracts from the forms of thought employed by the actors concerned in their deliberations. Secondly, parsimony in this case is bought at the price of closing off important areas of intellectual inquiry concerning the forms of thought employed by actors and the social conditions on which they depend.

2
The rational choice approach to social behaviour

This chapter provides a preliminary sketch of the basic structure of rational choice models and it surveys some influential applications of these models in public choice theory, the analysis of government taxation and spending policies, and the attempt to develop a game theoretical Marxism. We may begin with Downs's suggestion, in *An Economic Theory of Democracy*, that the abstract model of rational self-interested activity used so successfully in economic analysis can also be applied to other areas of social life. The model can be applied to the behaviour of private economic agents 'not because they are private but because they are agents. In short, they are human, and the realities of human nature must be accounted for in any economic analysis. Ipso facto, the same type of reasoning must be applied to every institution run by men' (Downs, 1957, p. 283). Consider just one example from Downs's discussion. Early studies of voting behaviour had found that a high proportion of voters were extremely ill-informed about politics, recognizing the names of few senior politicians, ignorant of the policy positions of the party they supported, and so on. This was frequently interpreted as a sign of the irrationality of voting behaviour. Downs shows, on the contrary, that given the costs of obtaining information and the low returns on any one person's vote such 'ignorance' on the part of voters may well be rational.

Downs assumes that individuals are utility maximizers. This means, first, that they make use of the most appropriate of the available means to pursue their ends and, secondly, that they exhibit a well-behaved preference structure: an actor preferring both A to B (a Labour to an Alliance government) and B to C (an Alliance to a Conservative government) will also prefer A to C. Since the publication of his book in 1957 a considerable amount of intellectual energy has been devoted to the analysis of politics and other areas of social life in terms of the actions of individuals who are rational in something like this sense. Of course, Downs and other advocates of the rational choice approach to the analysis of social life recognize that human behaviour frequently departs from the canons of rationality, so that rational choice models are not realistic. Downs refers us to Friedman's 'The methodology of positive economics' in support of his view that his models 'should be tested primarily by the accuracy of their predictions rather than by the reality of their assumptions' (p. 21). Friedman's argument is that models should be constructed so as to abstract 'the common and crucial elements from the mass of complex and detailed circumstances surrounding the phenomena to be explained' (Friedman, 1953, p. 14). The claim here is that unrealistic assumptions can nevertheless yield realistic predictions in so far as they are aimed at excluding what is inessential. There are serious methodological problems with such positivistic accounts of model-building, but these need not detain us here.[1]

There is a more sophisticated approach to the lack of realism of rational choice models, reminiscent of Weber's argument for the construction of ideal types of rational action. It suggests that the assumption of rationality provides the means of identifying the place of non-rational elements in human action. Hardin maintains that

> often the assumption of narrowly rational motivations yields predictions that are the most useful benchmark by which to assess the extent and the impact of other motivations. Occasionally it yields predictions which so nearly fit behaviour that investigation need go no further in order to satisfy us that we have understood why certain outcomes, and not others, occur.

The logic of collective action does just this in many contexts, although not in others. It yields a notoriously poor explanation of voting behaviour, since it suggests that almost no one would voluntarily vote in, say, American national elections. It helps us to understand why half of eligible Americans do not vote, but it does little to help us understand the other half. (Hardin, 1982, p. 11)

The lack of realism involved in the assumption of rationality, then, is treated either as a necessary simplification or else as providing a paradigm for the analysis of human behaviour in general. What Hardin means by the assumption of 'narrow' rationality is 'that individual actions are motivated by self-interest' (p.9). This is not the only understanding of rationality in the rational choice literature but it is certainly the most common. There is no suggestion that rational self-interest is the sole motivation of human action. The claim is rather that the assumption of 'narrow rationality' is the essential starting-point for analysis and that it may well have to be supplemented by consideration of other sources of action. Hardin refers to such extra-rational motivations as moral considerations and ignorance and misunderstanding. Other authors have suggested a more complex notion of rationality, and I consider some of their arguments below.

What are the implications of the assumption of narrow rationality for the analysis of social interaction and of collective outcomes? The most important point to notice here is that 'although it can make good sense to say that an individual is rational, there is no obviously new sense in which we can typically say that a group is rational' (Hardin, 1982, p. 2). I noted two components of Downs's assumption of rationality: the choice of appropriate means to pursue one's ends, and a preference structure exhibiting a certain consistency of choice. Neither component can be assumed at the level of a collective consisting of rational individuals. On the matter of preferences Arrow (1963) has shown that there is no reason in general to suppose that individual preferences can be aggregated into a well-defined collective preference structure. A considerable literature has since been devoted to exploring the problems of aggregating individual preferences into collective decisions.[2]

As for collective action, it is a mistake to suppose that rational individuals sharing an interest in a collective outcome can normally be expected to act so as to produce that outcome. This is most easily shown by means of the Prisoner's Dilemma. Imagine two prisoners who have collaborated in armed robbery. They have been picked up on suspicion and each is found to be in illegal possession of firearms. The police have insufficient evidence to convict them of the robbery and are conducting separate interrogations in the hope of obtaining a confession. The following deal is offered to each prisoner: if you confess and turn Queen's evidence we can put your partner away for eight years, and you can go free. If both confess the deal falls through, since neither's evidence against the other is necessary. They would then go down for six years. If neither confessed, the worst that could happen would be a short sentence for illegal possession.

It is not difficult to work out that if both are narrowly self-interested then both will confess. They both have an interest in neither confessing, but each would do better by confessing, whatever the other did. The prisoners fail to produce the most beneficial outcome for them because they are unable to communicate and because they face the dilemma once only. Change either of those conditions and the outcome might well be different. The significance of communication in this case is obvious. The dilemma as described above is unlikely to be repeated but there are many contexts in which we face repeated problems of collective action. These may generate incentives to co-operation that would not arise in a once-only interaction. Indeed, Taylor (1982) develops this point to provide accounts of socialization and of the emergence and perpetuation of social norms within a rational choice framework.

Nevertheless, the Prisoner's Dilemma provides a particularly clear example of a general feature of collective action. Just because all members of a group would benefit from the achievement of their common interests, it does not follow that they would act to achieve those interests. 'Indeed, unless the number of individuals in a group is quite small, or unless there is coercion or some other special device to make individuals act in their common interest, *rational self-interested individuals will not act to achieve their common or group interests'* (Olson, 1965, p. 2; emphasis in the original). If the group is small enough, an oligopoly for example, then the contribution of each individual can make a discernible difference to the furthering of their common interests, and the size of the group makes co-ordinated action a real possibility – unless, of course, that is ruled out by special conditions as in the Prisoner's Dilemma.

Neither consideration applies in the case of large groups, one of the larger trade unions, for example. The benefits of union organization are provided for each member (and sometimes for non-members in suitable employment) whether that member devotes time and energy to the union or not. The problem here is that there is no clear connection between the contribution of the individual member on the one hand and the strength of the union and the continued provision of the benefits that individual obtains from the existence of union organization on the other. The rational self-interested member, then, has no reason to incur the costs of contributing union dues, still less of active involvement in the organization. Olson therefore argues that a union or other organization that depends on voluntary contributions or the active commitment of at least some of its members, must provide its membership with additional incentives. These incentives may be of various kinds. Where membership is compulsory and where (as is normally the case in Britain) the employer deducts union dues from members' pay packets then there is no problem about collecting the dues. Olson cites a past president of the United Steel Workers of America describing an informal arrangement with similar effect:

> visual education...a high sounding label for a practice much more accurately described as dues picketing. It worked very simply. A group of dues-paying members, selected by the district director (usually more for their size than for their tact) would stand at the plant gate with pick handles or baseball bats in hand and confront each worker as he arrived for his shift. (McDonald, 1969, p. 121, quoted in Olson, 1982, p. 21)

For the more active minority, of course, other incentives are required. They may be motivated by a desire to win respect or friendship, or to be offered a managerial or supervisory position, or by a variety of other objectives.

Where there is no clear connection between the contribution of any one individual and the provision of some public good, then the rational self-interested individual has no incentive to contribute towards the provision of that good. 'A citizen receives the same protection from foreign invasion regardless of whether he has paid his taxes' (Rawls, 1972, p. 267). This situation defines what has become known as the free-rider problem. The free-rider obtains the benefits of a collective good without contributing towards its provision, in effect, by relying on the contributions of others. If there are too many free-riders then the quality of the good may be impaired, and it may not be provided at all. But why should the rational egoist be affected by that argument? Either the good will be provided at some level, or it will not – but the outcome will hardly be affected by the contribution of any one individual. Perhaps the most popular suggestion for avoiding the damaging consequences of free-riding has been some mechanism of social coercion. If national defence is a public good, then it must be paid for out of taxation, that is, out of compulsory contributions. The free-rider problem is one reason why rational egoists may favour state coercion to ensure the provision of valued public goods. Shortly after he quotes the illustration of the role of coercion in American union organization Olson notes that, as the free-rider argument implies, 'the same workers who had to be coerced to pay union dues voted for the unions with compulsory dues (and normally by overwhelming margins)' (Olson, 1982, p. 22).

There is certainly a problem of free-riders in a community of rational egoists but Olson goes further to suggest that the problem for large groups arises whether members are selfish or unselfish.

> Even if the member of a large group were to neglect his own interests entirely, he would still not rationally contribute toward the provision of any collective or public good, since his own contribution would not be perceptible. A farmer who placed the interests of other farmers above his own would not necessarily restrict his production to raise farm prices,

since he would know that his sacrifice would not bring a noticeable benefit to anyone. (Olson, 1982, p. 64)

It would be foolish to rely on voluntary contributions for the provision of many public goods: 'we do not voluntarily clean up our car exhausts or stop burning wood in our fireplaces; we seldom join our neighbors to clean up our blocks or to shovel snow from our alleys and sidewalks; we contribute, at most, trifling sums to collective causes we support, and most of us contribute nothing; most of us in the United States generally do not vote in most elections; fishing nations collectively destroy open-sea fisheries' (Hardin, 1982, p. 9).

THE RISE AND DECLINE OF NATIONS

Mancur Olson's *The Logic of Collective Action* was one of the most influential contributions to the modern development of the rational choice analysis of political life. *The Rise and Decline of Nations*, published in 1982, supplements and develops the implications of his earlier work. It too has had a considerable impact. It is of interest here as one of the most ambitious assertions of the explanatory pretensions of this style of analysis. In the preface Olson claims

> to extend existing economic theory in a way that not only explains the 'stagflation' and declining growth rates [of recent years] ... but also provides a partial explanation of a variety of problems usually reserved for other fields – the 'ungovernability' of some modern societies, the British class structure and the Indian caste system, the exceptionally unequal distribution of power and income in many developing countries, and even the rise of Western Europe from relative backwardness in the early Middle Ages to dominance of the whole world by the late nineteenth century. (Olson, 1982, p. ix)

To establish these claims Olson proposes to supplement the logic of his earlier book (1965) with some well-established elements of modern economics and he proceeds to draw out their implications in a series of nine abstract propositions. These provide the foundations for Olson's subsequent treatment of a wide range of substantive issues. For ease of reference they are all set out on page 74 of his book.

I have introduced Olson here in order to bring out the general character of his approach and of the claims he makes for it, so the details of his argument need not detain us. For present purposes, the essential point to notice is that he proposes to tackle the whole range of phenomena noted above in terms of the forms of collective action to be expected of rational individuals. In the first chapter, for example, we are told that this 'book shows for the first time how involuntary unemployment, and also deep depressions, can occur even when each decision-maker in the economy acts in accordance with his or her best interests' (Olson, 1982, p. 8).

The central argument of Olson's earlier book was that the existence of a large group with a common interest does not in itself give rise to collective action in pursuit of that interest. Collective action for large groups depends on the existence of selective incentives for those who join, and sometimes on an element of compulsion. Olson also shows that the situation of a small group is significantly different: its members can bargain with each other and compromise until they reach an optimal outcome. What happens if we apply these arguments to the analysis of national economies? To begin with, it is clear that there is no prospect of all the diverse interests working together to attain optimal outcomes through comprehensive bargaining. Many interests will not be organized at all, and there will be too many of those that are organized for the conditions of small group bargaining to apply. Such bargaining as does occur can be expected to defend the interests of the particular groups involved, rather than further the common interests of the whole society. Olson therefore draws the following conclusion (implication 4). 'On balance, special-interest organizations and collusions reduce efficiency and aggregate income in the societies in which they operate and make political life more divisive' (ibid., p. 74).

One important respect in which societies differ is in the extent and development of special interest organizations. The conditions of organization of small groups generally give them an advantage over large ones, but, given time and political stability, collective action organizations can be expected to develop for some of the larger groups. So we have this conclusion (implication 2): 'Stable societies with unchanged boundaries tend to accumulate more collusions and organizations for collective action over time' (ibid.).

These and other implications have an obvious relevance to the analysis of modern capitalist economies. They help to explain why Britain

> the major nation with the longest immunity from dictatorship, invasion, and revolution, has had in this century a lower rate of growth than other large, developed democracies. Britain has precisely the powerful network of special-interest organizations that the argument developed here would lead us to expect in a country with its record of military security and democratic stability. The number and power of its trade unions need no description. The venerability and power of its professional associations is also striking. (ibid., pp. 77–8)

Britain's experience is in marked contrast with those of France, West Germany and Japan, all of whom had their special-interest organizations much reduced by 'totalitarianism, instability, and war' (ibid., p. 79).[3]

The same set of principles accounts for the differential growth rates of parts of the United States, the rapid growth of the six founder members of the EEC, 'the growth of Britain and of Holland and (less clearly) of France in the early modern period and their roles in the rise of the once-backward civilization of Western Christendom ... the guild-ridden stagnation of the China that was first exposed to European pressure, not to mention the similar stagnation in India' (ibid., p. 235) – and much, much more besides. Olson is less certain about his theory's success in accounting for 'the British class structure, the Indian caste system, and the timing and character of the stronger forms of racial discrimination in South Africa' (ibid.), but he feels that it does a better job than any of the available alternatives.

Olson does not claim that his 'logic' and its nine 'implications' provide a complete account of the diverse phenomena he considers. But he clearly has little patience with *ad hoc* accounts of, say, Britain's relative economic decline – that is, with those accounts that rely on distinctive features of the society in question. Such *ad hoc* arguments are not necessarily false, but they are certainly insufficient because 'they are usually not testable against a broad enough array of data or experience to enable us to tell whether they are correct' (ibid., p. 10). The advantage of his own, more abstract approach is then that it can be tested against a wide range of conditions. In those terms it appears to be a great success. 'It is hard to see how it could explain so many diverse phenomena so simply if it were wholly or mainly false' (ibid., p. 236)

This last point brings out a feature that adherents of the rational choice approach find so attractive. Starting with a few abstract principles it generates theories that can be applied to the analysis of an enormous variety of situations. In this respect it appears both parsimonious and powerful. I argue that its parsimony is bought at too high a theoretical price and that its claims to explanatory power are largely spurious.

THE 'ECONOMICS OF POLITICS' AND PUBLIC CHOICE

This chapter began with Downs's claim that the treatment of agents as rational utility maximizers is relevant to all areas of social life, not merely to economic activity. *An Economic Theory of Democracy* represents an attempt to develop the implications of this view for the analysis of politics in democratic societies. Downs argues that economists have traditionally regarded government as 'that agency in the division of labour which has as its proper function the maximisation of social welfare' (Downs, 1957, p. 282). In other words, they have failed to treat government as a field of the self-interested activity of politicians.

The goal of politicians 'is to reap the rewards of holding office' and parties therefore 'formulate policies in order to win elections' (ibid., p. 28). Downs goes on to suggest that government decision-making is intended to maximize 'votes instead of utility or welfare' (p. 51). Riker, working in the same theoretical tradition, has noted that this last point involves a misleading analogy between entrepreneurs, who do seek to maximize profits, and politicians. To obtain the rewards of office politicians do not so much need to *maximize* votes, but rather to put together a minimum winning coalition (Riker, 1962). As for voters, they make decisions on the basis of calculations of costs, in the form of taxation, and benefits, in the form of 'streams of utility derived from government activity' (Downs, 1957, p. 36).

Since Downs's pioneering work there has developed a considerable literature applying the basic tenets of neo-classical economics to the analysis of political processes. This literature has been dominated by the 'public choice' school associated with the Center for the Study of Public Choice in Virginia and the journal *Public Choice*. Public choice theory, or the 'economics of politics', follows Downs's lead in developing accounts of the behaviour of politicians and of voters as rational self-serving agents, and it treats the behaviour of bureaucrats in similar terms.[4]

Much of this literature takes the form of an exposé of how government 'really' works – as the brief extracts from Downs's work will already have suggested. Where Olson maintains that relatively stable societies will be prey to the machinations of organized interests acting on government, the public choice school goes on to locate a problem of special interests within government itself. In his contribution to *The Economics of Politics* Buchanan presents the issue as follows. 'The challenge to us is one of constructing, or reconstructing, a political order that will channel the self-serving behaviour of participants towards the common good in a manner that comes as close as possible to that described for us by Adam Smith with respect to the economic order' (Buchanan *et al.*, 1978, p. 17).

To take just one example of the style of argument involved here consider the case of public expenditure. The general principle is straightforward: government directs its spending in order to win or maintain support, and finances that spending in ways that minimize the loss of support. Downs (1960) argued that budgets would tend to be too small. Voters would be all too aware of taxation and unclear about the uncertain and indirect benefits of government expenditure. They would therefore favour parties that promised to reduce government spending. Precisely the opposite conclusion can be obtained starting from the observation that many government spending programmes are targeted as a result of pressures from special interests. The benefits for the relevant interest group may be considerable, while the costs of any one programme are diffusely spread and represent at most a small increment to the general level of taxation. Government spending commitments and the general level of taxation will therefore tend to grow as parties compete for the support of various special interests.[5]

These opposed conclusions each presuppose a balanced budget, so that a spending commitment implies a corresponding tax imposition. If that assumption is relaxed we obtain an argument that democratic governments will tend to generate budget deficits, and therefore inflation (Buchanan and Wagner, 1977, Brittan, 1978). To generate a budget surplus requires an increase in taxation or a fall in expenditure. In either case a policy of budget surpluses will impose clear and observable losses on sections of the population, but no equally clear gains. Deficit financing, on the other hand, suggests to taxpayers 'that public services have become relatively cheaper. Because of these signals, voters will demand a shift in the composition of real output towards publicly provided services (including transfers)' (Buchanan and Wagner, 1977, pp. 103–4).

None of these arguments has been particularly successful in its empirical predictions. Democratic governments have at times been under pressure to increase public expenditure or to cut it back, and they have sometimes engaged in deficit financing. But the three accounts of public finance each suggest a pattern of development in government spending and finance that fails to correspond to the historical experience of Britain, the USA, or other societies to which they are supposed to apply (Toye, 1976, Tomlinson, 1981).

No matter. The differences between these positions are of interest for several reasons. First, they show how radically different conclusions can be generated from the same set of abstract principles as a result of different assumptions about the conditions in which they are supposed to apply. Once again, it would be a mistake to identify the rational choice approach, as a style of analysis, with any one of these conclusions. Secondly, the first two arguments differ mainly in the pressures on government spending and finance that they consider. In terms of the 'economics of politics' it is a weakness in each argument that it does not take account of the pressures considered in the other. The arguments combine to produce the following anodyne conclusion: government spending in a democracy will increase or decrease depending on the balance of forces acting on it.

Most interesting of all are the differences between the first two arguments and the third. It is not difficult to find *ad hoc* reasons (as Olson would have it) why politicians and electors in a given society might favour either balanced budgets or deficit financing, as the case may be. But there is no reason to suppose that a bias one way or the other should be expected to follow from the assumption that voters and politicians are both rational utility maximizers. In fact, as Tomlinson's (1981) discussion shows, the argument of Buchanan and Wagner is part of their polemic against the effects of Keynesian ideas. They wish to re-establish balanced budgets as 'the overriding constraint on public outlays' (Buchanan and Wagner, 1977, p. 176). Here is part of their explanation of why governments and voters have allowed that constraint to be relaxed.

> The Keynesian revolution began in the classroom and was nurtured there, but ultimately it invaded the citadels of power. The ideas of the Cambridge academic scribbler did modify, and profoundly, the actions of politicians and with precisely the sort of time lag that Keynes himself noted in the very last paragraph of his book. (ibid., p. 37)

The passage from Keynes's *General Theory* referred to here includes the following: 'the ideas of economists and political philosophers ... are more powerful than is commonly understood. Indeed the world is ruled by little else. Practical men who believe themselves to be quite exempt from any intellectual influences, are usually slaves of some defunct economist' (Keynes, 1936, p. 383). The analysis of politics as a realm of rational self-interested behaviour has to resort to a characteristically Keynesian conception of the influence of 'ideas' on economic policy.

Once the role of 'ideas' is admitted then the narrowly conceived 'economics of politics' must collapse. If conceptions of the desirability or otherwise of balanced budgets may be significant determinants of government action then politics cannot be seen as only a matter of self-interested activity. To take account of the role of ideas must require, at the very least, a more complex model of the individual actor than Downs and the public choice school appear to offer. Indeed, some rational choice analysts have developed models of political behaviour that try to take account of ideological commitments on the part of rational voters and political leaders.[6] I argue in later chapters that the role of ideas in political life has more damaging consequences for rational choice analysis than such modifications are able to admit.

THE NEW MARXISM OF COLLECTIVE ACTION

The last few years have seen the growth of what has been called 'the new Marxism of collective action' (Lash and Urry, 1984), which combines rational choice theory with versions of the traditional Marxist talk of exploitation, class struggle and the like. It appears in rather different forms in the work of Elster, Przeworski, Roemer and a growing number of others.[7] Roemer employs the mathematical tools of the theory of games to develop concepts of class and exploitation that escape the problems associated with Marx's theory of value. Przeworski provides extensive discussions of the development of social democratic politics in Western Europe, and Elster offers a wholesale reconstruction of Marx's social theory. These authors share a commitment to the analysis of social life in terms of an uncompromising methodological individualism. I shall comment briefly on the work of Elster and Przeworski to illustrate what is at stake here.

In *Making Sense of Marx* Elster sets out to show that what remains of value in Marx's work must be understood in terms of methodological individualism. In these terms much of what is commonly regarded as central to Marxism has to go: Marx's theory of value and much of his economic analysis, functional and teleological explanation, and methodological collectivism. This last involves the assumption that 'there are supra-individual entities that are prior to the individual in the explanatory order' (Elster, 1985, p. 6). On that assumption individual action would be explained in terms of an aggregate pattern. There are, for example, passages in Marx's *Capital* where he treats capitalists as mere personifications of portions of capital, so that their actions are determined as a function of their position in the total social capital. Or again, Marx and later Marxists frequently indulge in methodologically collectivist accounts of classes and the struggles between them – as if classes as such were actors on the political stage.

Elster's fundamental objection to methodological collectivism is that it is incompatible with the intentional analysis of human action. What remains of central importance in Marx's work once the collectivist dross has been removed is his critique of exploitation and alienation and, in particular, his pioneering explanations in terms of the unintended consequences of human action. The causal explanation of aggregate phenomena in terms of the individual actions that go into them 'is the specifically Marxist contribution to the methodology of the social sciences' (Elster, 1985, p. 4). How can this methodological individualism be reconciled with the structural analyses of capitalist economic life that play such an important part in Marx's mature work?

Elster deals with this issue by means of a surreptitious structural determination of actors' forms of thought. He maintains that there is a valuable core in Marx's theory of ideology, namely, that it 'involves an understanding of the whole from the point of view of the part' (ibid., p. 476). There are two rather different mechanisms here, one of which leads members of a class to confuse their interests with the interests of society as a whole. The idea of class interests is a highly contentious issue in Marxist thought and Elster devotes surprisingly little attention to disputes over its interpretation. No matter. Here is how he defines class:

> A class is a group of people who by virtue of what they possess are compelled to engage in the same activities if they want to make the best use of their endowments. (ibid., p. 331)[8]

Since Elster defines rationality in terms of maximizing behaviour, this amounts to saying that what is to count as rational for members of a class is determined by their class position. On this point, Marx's valuable core consists of the suggestion that people generalize from their own class interests to those of the rest of society. Why actors who are assumed to be rational in other respects should be blinkered in this way remains unclear.

The second mechanism is the cognitive fallacy of generalizing from relations that are valid only locally. The significance of this point for Elster's reconstruction of Marx's thought is 'that unintended consequences arise when agents entertain beliefs about each other that exemplify the fallacy of composition' (p. 48). Indeed, Elster describes that idea as 'Marx's central contribution to the methodology of the social sciences' (ibid.). Suppose that one capitalist enterprise succeeds in reducing its wages while the others continue as before. The result will be that its profits increase. If all capitalists reduce wages in order to increase profits, the result will be that wages and the general level of profits both fall. What seems like rational action at the level of each enterprise has damaging results in the aggregate:

> we must indeed expect something to give if each capitalist acts on an assumption – that only his workers should save or accept lower wages – which as a matter of logic cannot be true for all. (ibid., p. 26)

In this way, Elster suggests, tendencies at the level of the economy as a whole can be explained as the unintended consequences of an aggregate of individually rational decisions.

' This mechanism generates social change not only in capitalism, but in any society in which economic decisions suffer from lack of co-ordination' (ibid.).

There are at least two problems here. One concerns the limited notion of rationality. In Elster's example, each enterprise acts on the assumption that others will continue as before, that is, it acts rationally on the basis of irrational assumptions about the behaviour of other capitalists. Why are they all so foolish? Elster's argument requires that capitalist enterprises are constrained to act in that way by virtue of the way they perceive their situation, which in turn is a function of their social location as capitalists. Here too what is to count as rational is determined by the actor's social situation.

The other problem concerns the use of 'unintended consequences' as an explanatory device. It is a commonplace of Western social thought both that actions have unintended consequences, and that they do so no matter what beliefs actors entertain about each other. What Elster presents as 'Marx's central contribution' is a trivial consequence. If that is what Marx has to offer it is difficult to see why Elster should write a book about him, let alone such a large one.

Why make such a fuss about the banal tale of the unintended consequence? The answer, of course, lies in a problem that always confronts methodological individualism in its attempts to deal with structural features of social relationships. The intentional analysis of individual action is one thing, and the analysis of recurrent patterns of interaction and other structural features of social life is quite another. For methodological individualism the tale of the unintended consequence operates as a more general version of the economists' hidden hand, and with much the same result. It is a marvellously flexible device for appearing to reduce one level of analysis to another. In the absence of some surreptitious determination of actors' forms of thought by their social location the idea that an aggregation of unintended consequences could explain anything about social structure would be an absurdity.

Przeworski (1985) also insists on an uncompromising methodological individualism in his examination of the development of West European socialist movements. One set of arguments

examines the consequences for a socialist movement of the
decision to enter the parliamentary and electoral arenas. The
effect of that choice is to lock the socialist movement into the
logic of party competition. The crucial feature of this logic for
a socialist party is the requirement it imposes to aim at electoral
majorities under conditions in which a large minority at most
is directly susceptible to a socialist class appeal. The pursuit
of electoral majorities therefore involves some dilution of
socialist principles and direct appeal to working-class interests.
Furthermore, Przeworski argues, the division of society into
classes does not necessarily entail the organization of politics
in terms of class struggle. The political salience of class is
itself 'a cumulative consequence of the strategies pursued by
political parties of the Left' (Przeworski and Sprague, 1986,
p. 9). More precisely, it is a consequence of the success of
those strategies in countering the strategies of their political
opponents. Class is salient

> if, when, and only to the extent to which it is important
> to political parties which mobilize workers. Workers are the
> only potential proponent of the class organization of politics
> – when no political forces seek to mobilize workers as a class,
> separately from and in opposition to all other classes, class
> is absent altogether as.a principle of political organization.
> (ibid., pp. 10–11)

The other set of arguments considers the question of whether
workers' pursuit of their material interests will lead them to
opt for socialism. Even if we were to assume that socialism
would be better than capitalism at satisfying workers' material
interests, there would still be conditions in which it was rational
of workers to prefer capitalism. First, the period of transition
to socialism may well involve some deterioration in living
conditions. Secondly, it may be possible to establish a class
compromise in which low levels of wage militancy are offered
in return for high and reliable levels of capitalist investment.
In effect, the argument is that it would be irrational of workers
in capitalist democracies to prefer socialism under conditions of
successful corporatism. Przeworski concludes that the pursuit of

material interests within the conditions of capitalist democracy
may well be desirable, but that it should not be confused with
the struggle for socialism.

Przeworski's arguments bring together two strains of political
analysis. On the one hand he insists that classes are not
collective actors and that individuals do indeed make choices –
that is, their behaviour is not the acting out of an internalized
society. Social relations should be treated 'as structures of
choices available to actors, not as sources of norms to be
internalized and acted' (Przeworski, 1985, p. 96). On the other
hand he continues to write of classes and class struggle. Classes
are no longer regarded as given in the structure of property
relations. Rather they 'are formed as effects of struggles; as
classes struggle they transform the conditions under which
classes are formed' (ibid., p. 92).

Now, it follows from Przeworski's methodological individualism that classes are not collective actors, and therefore that
classes as such do not struggle. What he refers to as struggles
between classes must therefore be understood as something
altogether more complex – in which ideas of classes and their
conflicting interests play an important part in the choices of
individuals. The claim that agencies of collective action are
themselves formed in part as a result of struggle is, of course,
entirely acceptable. But why should we understand those agencies, or some of them, in terms of classes? The answer is that
in spite of his insistence on the formation of classes in struggle,
Przeworski continues to treat interests as given in the structure
of property relations. All those who are separated from the
means of production are forced to sell their labour power in
return for wages. 'This produces a commonality of interests
defined in terms of a number of secondary characteristics,
particularly of a distributional nature, and leads to the notion
of the working people' (ibid., p. 91). It is presumably in terms
of those interests that Przeworski and Sprague, in a passage
quoted above, can write of workers as 'the only potential
proponent of the class organization of politics' (1986, p. 11;
emphasis added).

Unfortunately, once interests are identified in this way as
given by actors' social locations, then the choices of rational

actors are given by those interests and the conditions of action they confront. Przeworski's insistence on the importance of actors' *choices*, like Elster's tale of the unintended consequence, serves merely to cover a surreptitious structural determination. The choices and their consequences that Przeworski discusses are those of idealized rational actors endowed with ends given by the circumstances that confront them.

3

Rationality, egoism and social atomism

One of the appeals of the rational choice approach lies in its claim to produce powerful results starting from a few relatively simple assumptions. This chapter examines those assumptions and shows how they depend on a distinctive model of the human actor and a reductionist treatment of structural features of social life. We may begin with the characterization proposed by Hollis (1979a) as the basis for his critical discussion. Hollis notes three fundamental assumptions. First, actors are rational and their rationality is understood in strictly utilitarian terms. Actors have a given set of ends, they choose between them in a consistent fashion, and they select from the available means of action those most appropriate to the realization of their chosen ends. In this sense of rationality, the ends themselves are neither rational nor irrational, they are simply there. Secondly, actors are assumed to be narrowly self-interested. Thirdly, they are social atoms: 'they could be picked at random from their groups, because it made no difference *who* they were' (ibid., p. 6). They are human individuals, but they are not regarded as essentially located within a social structure of positions and roles.

We shall see that these assumptions may be relaxed in some respects without damage to the rational choice approach, but they do provide a useful starting-point for our discussion. Hollis disputes all three assumptions, by raising the question of the rationality of ends, by a limited endorsement of the idea of *homo sociologicus*, who is neither consistently selfish nor a social atom, and by questioning the Humean proposition that only desire can motivate action (Hollis, 1981, 1983). The assumption of atomism is closely related to a methodological individualism which Hollis does not question. We consider each of these assumptions in turn.

To get a clear understanding of the notion of rationality employed in rational choice analysis it is necessary to start with the idea of maximizing behaviour. It is difficult to be clear what this involves without some use of symbols. Here I follow the brief account by Hahn and Hollis (1979) in their introduction to *Philosophy and Economic Theory*. Suppose that an actor faces a choice amongst a number of possible courses of action. In order to speak of that choice in terms of maximizing behaviour it is necessary to assume that the various outcomes can be compared according to some common standard. More precisely, let c, c', c", etc., be the set of consequences of the actor's possible actions, and let R be a relation between members of that set, with cRc' meaning 'c is at least as good as c' '. It is possible to speak of choice as maximizing if the following conditions hold:

(1) completeness; for all pairs (c,c') either cRc' or c'Rc or both
(2) reflexivity; for all c, cRc
(3) transitivity; for every (c,c',c"), if cRc', and c'Rc", then cRc".

If (1) does not hold then there will be outcomes that cannot be compared by the relation 'at least as good as'. If (2) or (3) do not hold then 'at least as good as' yields no consistent pattern of preferences. We can now define rational choice as follows.

> Given the set of available actions, the agent chooses rationally if there is no other action available to him the consequence of which he prefers to that of the chosen action. (Hahn and Hollis, 1979, p. 4)

Since we are concerned with choice as resulting in action it is necessary to add that a rational action is one that expresses a rational choice. This relation between reason and action is sometimes referred to as behavioural rationality (Macdonald and Pettit, 1981, chapter 2). It is one component of the notion of rationality we are now discussing.

A second component is that the actor's preferences are assumed to be given. This does not mean that the preferences cannot be explained or that they may not change. Preferences are normally regarded as a function of an underlying set of beliefs and desires and of the situation of choice or action confronting the actor. The point of treating preferences as given in assessing the rationality or otherwise of action is that the assessment has nothing to do with the substance of the actor's preferences. It is just a matter of the relations between those preferences, and between choice and action. There are two important points to be made here. First, on this view of rationality there is no sense in which the rationality of the preferences themselves can be put in question either in terms of their relationship to some substantive ethical or other standards, or in terms of the way the preferences have been formed. Given preferences and the relations between them then the rational choice follows in much the way that the conclusion to an argument follows from its premises.

There is no space in this view of rationality either for the Weberian topic of substantive rationality[1] or for a broader sense of individual rationality as embracing individual autonomy and responsibility for oneself. What is involved in this broader view of rationality is the idea that people's preferences and other characteristics at particular times are partly a consequence of their own past choices and of how they have chosen to conduct their lives. In that sense we are responsible for at least some of our own future preferences.[2] Those who act rationally in terms of what their current preferences happen to be, may nevertheless conduct themselves irrationally in terms of a view of rationality as having application over a longer period.

The second point to notice is that preferences may well change. For example, they may change in response to advertising, political campaigning, or fashion trends. Or again, taking up my last point, actors may have 'preferences' about their own preferences (Sen, 1977a, 1983, Hirschman, 1982). They may prefer to have preferences which would enable them to give up smoking, to eat or drink less, or to get up earlier in the morning. In such cases, preference change involves 'a battle with oneself that is marked by all kinds of feints, ruses, and strategic devices' (Hirschman, 1982, p. 71). Provided that the overall pattern of preferences remains relatively stable, there is no reason why rational choice analysis need be threatened by such changes.

A final component of this notion of rationality is that preferences are assumed to be homogeneous, in the sense that any two can be compared in terms of the relation 'at least as good as'. Actors can compare the life of a contented pig with that of a discontented Socrates and decide that one is at least as good as the other. They can compare pushpin with poetry and reach a decision – if only that they are indifferent between them. They can also compare a reduction in taxation with, say, a cutback in expenditure on education or the social services. This assumption of homogeneity has been disputed in several ways. I referred above to Sen's argument that actors may have preferences about their preferences – so that not all their preferences can be treated as if they were on the same level. Others, as we shall see in a moment, have disputed the assumption of egoism, arguing that actors may also have preferences that are not strictly self-interested.

To conclude this section, I have noted three components of the notion of rationality in rational choice analysis: behavioural rationality, and preferences that are both given and homogeneous. Action is not always rational in this sense, and no-one claims that it is. I have also indicated ways in which it could be argued that this notion of rationality endows the actor 'with too little structure' (Sen, 1977a, p. 235); actors may work to change their preferences and their preferences are not necessarily homogeneous. Now, it is important to be clear that these points in themselves do no damage to the claims of rational choice analysis. In the first part of chapter 2 I quoted Hardin to the effect that 'the assumption of narrowly rational motivations yields predictions that are the most useful benchmark by which to assess the extent and the impact of other motivations' (Hardin, 1982, p. 11). The claim, in other words, is not that action is invariably rational, in the sense just discussed, but rather that the assumption of rationality is a necessary starting-point for identifying the place of other motivations in social life. Or, as Elster puts the same point,

> although there are strong reasons in principle to insist on the distinctions between intentionality and rationality, and between rationality and optimality, explanation in terms of optimization remains the paradigm case of intentional explanation in the social sciences outside psychology. (1983a, p. 75)

Why should rational, optimizing behaviour be accorded this paradigmatic status? I return to this question in chapter 4.

EGOISM

Numerous critics have pointed to the assumption of egoism as an obvious weakness of the rational choice approach. Everyday experience and experimental results on behaviour in Prisoners' Dilemma games both suggest that, as Sen puts it, people 'frequently do the unselfish thing' (1977a, p. 341). One possibility is that actors are not always sufficiently sophisticated to realize that selfishness is the only rational approach. Another is that recurrent patterns of interaction involve a pattern of costs and incentives different to once-only interaction, so that actors take account of the future implications of their present choices. Both these possibilities may be assimilated without too much difficulty into the rational choice model. Sen notes a further possibility 'that the person is *more* sophisticated than the theory allows and that he has asked himself what type of preference he would like the other player to have, and on somewhat Kantian grounds has considered the case for himself having those preferences, or behaving *as if* he had them' (ibid.).

Most work in the rational choice tradition does indeed equate rationality with the pursuit of self-interest, but this need not be interpreted narrowly. Concern for the sufferings of others may figure along with one's own pleasures in the actor's judgements of 'at least as good as'. What matters for the rational choice model is that all preferences are comparable, not that they are narrowly self-interested. Sen makes an important distinction here between 'sympathy' and 'commitment'. Both go against the idea of egoism in certain respects, but sympathy, in which the sufferings of others are experienced as upsetting and therefore as affecting one's own welfare, can be readily integrated within the rational choice approach. Commitment is more difficult to deal with. It provides a motive for choices that may run counter to the welfare of the chooser. In effect, Sen avoids the identification of rationality with egoism by endowing the actor with more than one preference order.

Schick (1984) presents a rather different argument to similar effect. He defines rational choice as one that maximizes not preferences but rather the actor's expected utility and goes on to insist that people also act for reasons that are not rational in this narrow sense. They may act on 'social' grounds, as when a person 'accommodates (or crosses) others because he sees who they are and what it is they want' (p. 89) – that is, they may do that without reference to their own expected utility. Social action may involve commitment to an ideal, to an ethical (or other) principle, but it need not do so. 'Not every reason is rational, and there may sometimes be social reasons where there are no rational ones. Reasons go beyond rationality, and so the range of action does too' (p. 148).

The claim that there are significant motivations other than narrowly self-interested ones suggests that the standard rational choice model endows the actor 'with too little structure' (Sen, 1977a, p. 235). What is required to remedy that shortcoming is presumably more structure. Sen (1983) proposes a ranking of preference rankings. Margolis proposes to integrate altruism into the rational choice framework precisely by endowing the actor with a little more structure. His actors have both an altruistic and an egoistic preference order, and an allocation mechanism which determines what proportion of the actor's resources will be devoted to self-interested or altruistic ends. Notice that, in these examples, the supposed inadequacy of the assumption of egoism is dealt with by proposing a somewhat more complex model of the internal structure of the actor – not by reference to the normative or other discourses within which the actor's calculations are embedded.

Finally, as I noted in connection with the assumption of rationality, rational choice theory does not deny the existence of other motivations. The claim is rather that the presumption of rational self-interested action provides the starting-point for analysis, which may well be forced to recognize the role of other motivations. Hardin notes that the assumption of narrow rationality 'helps us to understand why half of eligible Americans do not vote, but it does little to help us understand the other half' (1982, p. 11). Later in the same book he argues that extra-rational considerations do indeed play a part in collective action:

> a peculiar implication of the logic of collective action is that so little large-scale collective action *can be* narrowly rational that, indeed, very little *is* narrowly rational; thus even perfunctory moral concern at the mass level may stimulate more collective action than self-interest does. Anyone trying to explain political activity may then be led to think that morality is relatively important as compared with self-interest. But ... this conclusion about the role of moral choice in the politics of the mass may be based on undue consideration of activity, when the more pervasive phenomenon may be explainable inactivity. (ibid., p. 124)

The critic of rational choice analysis has to do more than note the existence of non-self-interested motivations.

SOCIAL ATOMISM

I began this chapter by noting that Hollis (1979a) presents the rational choice approach as treating actors as social atoms. They differ from each other only in the interests which arise from the situations (capitalist, worker, or whatever) in which they find themselves and in the skill with which they pursue those interests. As he describes it atomism is certainly a form of methodological individualism, but Hollis's objection concerns a rather different point, as we shall see in a moment.

Discussions of methodological individualism frequently confuse two rather different debates.[3] One concerns the autonomy of the individual *vis-à-vis* supra-individual entities. The debate here is between an insistence on the irreducibility of individual decision and action and what Elster calls methodological collectivism. The other concerns the question of reductionism, the idea that social life is reducible to the constitutive actions of individual actors. The debate here concerns the sense in which actors can be said to be dependent on social conditions of various kinds: are they isolated atoms or essentially social? If action depends on conditions that are social in the minimal sense of being external to the actor, then social life is not reducible to the constitutive actions of the actors involved.

Hollis disputes both the atomism of rational choice models and the 'sociological' alternative in which actors are treated as creatures of their social location. In his view, rationality 'has to consist in identifying with some set of principles neither merely because one wants to nor merely because they are the going norms of one's station but because, whatever it may mean to say so, they are in one's real interest' (Hollis, 1979a, p. 13). Precisely what is at stake in Hollis's notion of 'real interest' remains unclear since, unlike the usual notion of interests, they are not a simple function either of current preferences or of social location. As against such accounts of interests, Hollis suggests that 'the rational man needs an identity in which he can be fully *himself*' (ibid. p. 12), and again that 'it may be in one's real interest to affirm an identity' (ibid., p. 13). 'Real interest' here is clearly a surrogate for individual autonomy or free will. It implies a source of motivation that is reducible neither to desire nor to social structure. His objection to the atomism of rational choice analysis is directed against its simplistic account of actors' motivations, not against its reductionism.

Now, rational choice analysis combines a rejection of methodological collectivism with a treatment of actors as social atoms. In this respect it accords a very limited role to the significance of social structure or social relations for actors and their actions. This point can be brought out most clearly in terms of the 'new Marxism of collective action' which attempts to combine Marxism's emphasis on the structural characteristics of capitalism with an insistence on the primacy of individual choice in the explanation of social life.

I referred in chapter 2 to Elster's opposition to methodological collectivism, the assumption that 'there are supra-individual entities that are prior to the individual in the explanatory order' (1985, p. 6). Elsewhere (Elster, 1978, 1979) he produces powerful and effective arguments against those functionalist and structuralist positions which insist on 'the primacy of structural constraints' in the determination of individual action. In contrast to these positions he insists that social processes and the actions of collectivities are always in principle reducible to the actions of human individuals. In effect, he runs together the two debates distinguished above by suggesting that the only alternatives for social theory are either an individualistic reductionism or a methodological collectivism.[4] There are two further assumptions to notice in Elster's account of the actor. One is that action is a function of decisions made by actors in pursuit of their preferences, whatever they happen to be, and the other is that actors are human individuals. Hollis questions the first of these, as we have seen, but not the second. Both will be disputed in the following chapters.

Now, the effect of an individualistic reductionism is that social structure enters the argument in two ways. First, structural features of social life are themselves the 'unintended consequences' of an aggregate of individual actions. Secondly, structural effects enter into the explanation of action only to the extent either that they affect the (past) conditions in which the actor's current preferences were formed, or that they provide the conditions in which action now takes place. In other words, 'structural' conditions determine the opportunities, incentives and costs that individuals have to confront in deciding on a course of action. Przeworski presents this view of social structure as follows:

> social relations are treated as structures of choices available to actors, not as sources of norms to be internalized and acted. Social relations are the structures within which actors, individual and collective, deliberate upon goals, perceive and evaluate alternatives, and select courses of action. As

a corollary, let me repeat ... that social relations must themselves be viewed as a historically contingent outcome of, to use Marx's phrase again, 'men's reciprocal actions'. (1985, p. 96)

The last two sentences are unexceptionable. The trouble with the idea that social relations are the outcome, or the unintended consequences, of past actions is not that it is wrong, but rather that it is uninformative.

The difficulty with Przeworski's position comes with the first sentence. It is one thing to regard social relations as the conditions in which actors choose. Who could possibly wish to deny it? It is quite another to regard them as the available choices themselves – as if the set of available choices is given in the social situation of the actor. The difference is a matter of the process of assessment and evaluation of the situation of action leading up to whatever choice the actor makes. To treat the available choices as given in the pattern of social relations is, in effect, to deny the role of that process. Similarly, Elster argues that there is 'an important core of truth in the idea that opportunities are central in the explanation of behaviour, since preferences themselves are to a large extent shaped by what is possible' (Elster, 1985, p. 20). To suggest that actors' preferences are largely given by their circumstances is to deny any significant role to the forms of thought employed by actors in their evaluations and assessments.

Now, Elster, Przeworski and other exponents of rational choice Marxism present the issue as if the only alternative to atomism were a methodological collectivism in which individual action is to be understood as a consequence of some overarching structural determination. On the one side is the view of the human individual as creative subject, pursuing its interests to the best of its ability and constituting actions and social relations in the process – albeit under conditions that are given rather than freely chosen. On the other is the picture of the human subject as literally subjected to the system of social relations in which it internalizes its part and subsequently acts it out.

In fact, for all their apparent opposition these views of the actor have much in common. Both involve what I shall call a portfolio model of the actor. In this model action is seen as resulting from the interaction of the situation of action and the actor's more or less stable 'portfolio' of beliefs and desires. In rational choice models the desires themselves are supposed to have a utilitarian structure, so that optimal outcomes are normally well defined and action generally takes the form of maximizing behaviour. What produces action in any given case is the actor's rational assessment of the situation in the light of its beliefs and desires. The individualism of this position is little more than a matter of insisting that actors do indeed make choices and act on them. The structural or collectivist alternatives adopt much the same model of the actor, and add that the content of the portfolio is internalized as a function of the actor's social location.

In both cases actors are creatures of their situations and they act accordingly: in one case because they pursue the most rational course of action given the situation in which they find themselves and in the other because they have internalized the appropriate norms and act on them. In fact, we have seen that it would not be difficult to develop an account of the emergence and perpetuation of norms within a rational choice framework once the nature of incentives involved in repeated patterns of interaction are taken into consideration.[5] The mechanism by which individuals are subordinated to their situations may be different in the two cases, but the overall result is the same.

But there is another sense in which the rational choice approach imposes severe 'structural' constraints on the choices of individuals. At one level 'rationality' involves little more than a certain consistency of choice, each actor being characterized by a coherent decision rule that is always followed. However, no rational choice analysis operates with such a general and unrestricted notion of rationality. The construction of explanatory models requires not only that actors are normally rational in this sense, but also that all actors within certain categories are rational in essentially the same way. For example, if a model contains two categories of actor, consumers and capitalist entrepreneurs, then the model assumes that the former are all characterized by preference sets with the same mathematical structure and that the latter are all profit maximizers in a sense that is similarly defined for all entrepreneurs. This last assumes a single well-defined notion of what is to count as capital and as profit, and the same set of decision procedures and time-scale of calculation in all cases.

Now, there is considerable evidence to show that several quite distinct modes of economic calculation may be employed by firms operating within a single national economy.[6] The coexistence of distinct modes of calculation may pose practical difficulties for the construction of workable mathematical models of market co-ordination, but it need not imply that some modes of calculation are less rational than others. The point here is that a uniquely defined mode of economic calculation (profit maximizing) cannot be deduced from the postulate of rationality alone. In effect, rational choice models require a general presumption of rationality on the part of actors, and a further, surreptitious postulate that what is to count as rationality is uniquely defined for each category of actor recognized by the model.

At first sight that procedure may not appear too problematic. After all, if we notice that capitalists do not all employ the same mode of calculation then, of course, the model can be complicated to take account of the different modes of profit-seeking that can be identified.[7] There is no difficulty for rational choice theory in taking account of differences in the way members of distinct social categories assess their situations of action. The theoretical problem lies elsewhere, in the assumption that the forms of assessment employed by actors (that is, what is to count as rationality for those actors) are determined by the social categories to which they belong. In effect, the construction of rational choice models presupposes a 'structural' determination of the forms of thought employed by actors, in so far as they are rational.

Readers will have noticed the presence in this section of terms such as 'forms of thought', 'modes of calculation' and 'process of evaluation'. These terms did not appear in the expositional sections of the previous chapter or in my discussion of the presumption of rationality. The reason is that actors' deliberations play no significant part in the construction of models in rational choice analyses. Nor do they play a significant part in accounts of action as a function of internalized norms and values. My discussion here assumes that deliberation will sometimes be an important part of the process of choice. Hollis is entirely justified in his view that action is not always reducible to the pursuit of desire or the acting out of internalized norms, but there is no need to invoke a mysterious notion of 'real interest' in support of that view. The implications of deliberation will play an important part in the arguments of the following chapters.

4
Models of the actor

We have seen that rational choice analyses depend on a number of basic assumptions. These involve a model of the individual actor and an account of the structure of social relations in which actors are located. The model of the actor combines two rather different senses of rationality. One concerns the connection between actors' choices and their actions: action is the expression or realization of a choice by the actor. This has been called 'behavioural rationality' (Macdonald and Pettit, 1981). The other concerns the mental state or character of the actor: actors' choices themselves result from a 'rational' structure of preferences regarding the outcomes of possible actions. In effect, it is assumed that any two outcomes may be compared in terms of the relation 'at least as good as' and that that relation is transitive. Now, the set of possible outcomes facing the actor will change from one situation to another, so that actors' preferences regarding outcomes will also change. Since the point of constructing models of rational choice is to be able to consider what actors might do in a number of situations, it is usual to relate an actor's preferences to an underlying set of beliefs and desires. Those beliefs and desires that have a bearing on the situation of action currently facing the actor then determine what the actor's preferences are in that situation. 'Rationality' in this second sense involves a set of beliefs and desires such that the actor has a 'rational' preference structure in most situations.

Rational choice analysis usually goes further than these basic assumptions in at least two respects. The first is an assumption of egoism. Actors' preferences are ordered by the relation 'at least as good as' and it is not unreasonable to suppose that actors have some self-regarding preferences. This suggests that egoism might be the common property of actors' preferences that makes their ordering possible. Egoism, in this general sense, need not be interpreted too narrowly. Actors may be pained by the sufferings of others, in which case their egoism does not exclude an element of sympathy. We have seen that several critics argue for a more complex model of the actor, involving motivations that are not egoistic even in this sense.

Secondly, the construction of the formal deductive models that are the distinctive feature of this approach depends on a further, usually surreptitious postulate. This is that what is to count as rationality is uniquely defined for each category of actor recognized by the model. This means, for example, that all entrepreneurs will be profit maximizers in a sense that is similarly defined for all members of that category. The reason why this last postulate is generally surreptitious is that it suggests that actors' forms of thought are determined by the social category to which they belong. In effect, it is a form of structural determinism which conflicts with the explicit commitment to methodological individualism of most versions of rational choice theory. Individuals, we are told, should not be seen as the mere creatures of their positions in some overarching social structure. On the contrary, the structural features of social life are themselves products of the constitutive actions of human individuals. Social structure, on this account, does not so much determine action as provide for each actor the pattern of costs, incentives and opportunities that characterize the situation in which action is to take place.

Nobody, of course, would pretend that this model of the actor was entirely realistic. Rational choice analysis makes two related claims. One is that this model is capable of generating powerful explanatory hypotheses across a wide range of social conditions and types of behaviour. The other is that the point at which the model proves to be inadequate is the point at which other motivations must be brought into play – precisely to deal with the action or actions that cannot be accounted for on the assumption of rationality. In effect, the claim here is that the model of rational choice has a paradigmatic, indeed a normative status in the analysis of human behaviour. This second claim would not be plausible without the first. If the assumptions of the model were not thought to be so successful, they could hardly provide the norm against which other accounts of behaviour were to be measured.

This chapter discusses models of the actor. The rational choice model may be regarded as refining, that is, as imposing further restrictions on, models that are more general. The following section introduces the most general and abstract concept of actor. A first refinement of this concept gives a model that regards action as resulting from the actor's rational application of a more or less stable set of beliefs and desires. Given the situation of action the actor selects from its portfolio of beliefs and desires those that seem relevant, and uses them to decide on a course of action. I call that the portfolio model of the actor. The rational choice model makes a further refinement of the portfolio model, with the assumption that the actor's set of desires has a utilitarian structure. The result of this assumption is that an optimal outcome can be identified in most situations confronting the actor. Rational action then takes the form of optimizing behaviour. The utilitarian assumption is an integral part of rational choice analysis, but the portfolio model is more widely used. This chapter provides a general account of the portfolio model and its implications for intentional analysis, and it shows that there is nothing in that model to justify the paradigmatic status claimed for the model of rational choice.

Chapter 5 takes the argument further, using critical discussion of the portfolio model to raise more general theoretical questions concerning the rationality of action. I argue that the treatment of actors as by and large rational, and as acting in terms of a more or less stable portfolio of beliefs and desires has the effect of obscuring important questions of the forms of thought employed by actors in assessing their situations and deciding on courses of action. Chapter 6 develops the implications of these arguments for the analysis of structural features of social life.

A MINIMAL CONCEPT OF THE ACTOR

An actor is a locus of decision and action, where the action is in some sense a consequence of the actor's decisions. Actors do things as a result of their decisions. We call those things actions, and the actor's decisions play a part in their explanation. Actors may also do things that do not result from their decisions, and their explanation has a different form. This is a minimal concept of the actor. Most accounts of the actor build considerably more into their model than I have provided here. Actors are characterized by their possession of a more or less stable portfolio of beliefs and desires, more often than not they are assumed to be human beings, and in rational choice models they are supposed to possess a utilitarian structure of preferences. Giddens, who is far from advocating the rational choice approach, suggests that one of the problems with the analysis of action in terms of intentions, reasons and so on, is that it tends to abstract from features that are central to human activity:

> 'Action' is not a combination of 'acts': 'acts' are constructed only by a discursive moment of attention to the durée of lived-through experience. Nor can action be discussed in separation from the body, its mediations with the surrounding world and the coherence of the acting self. (Giddens, 1984, p. 3)

Here what I call the portfolio model is taken up and modified by the addition of yet more assumptions.

The minimal concept of actor incorporates none of the further assumptions noted in the last paragraph. It says that a capacity to make decisions is an integral part of anything that might be called an actor, and it says that those decisions may have consequences. Other entities, like the moon or the river Thames, do things but they would not normally be described as making decisions and acting on them. This concept is formal and abstract. It tells us nothing about the conditions that make it possible for something to be an actor, except that it must be capable of reaching decisions and of acting on some of them. By the same token it says nothing about the other characteristics that actors may possess. To say that actors' decisions play a part in their actions is not to deny that other conditions might also be involved in the determination of action – for example, that processes of which the actors are unconscious might play a part in human activities.

In effect, this abstract concept of actor is organized around the idea of what has been called 'behavioural rationality', the idea that action expresses a choice. Unlike the model of rational choice or other versions of the portfolio model it imposes no further restrictions on what may count as an actor. Human individuals are normally actors in this sense, but they are clearly not the only entities that make decisions and act on them. Depending on how 'decision' and related terms are understood it may not be reasonable to suppose that 'behavioural rationality is a prerogative of human beings ... for we take other mammals to be moved to action by a similar pressure of belief and desire: the dog runs towards the gate, we assume, because it believes that doing so is a way of getting the ball, something it manifestly wants' (Macdonald and Pettit, 1981, p. 59). In this case the question of what distinguishes human actors from other animal actors would be a matter of what further attributes are involved over and above some capacity to make decisions and act on them.

More important for the argument of this book is a different set of actors other than human individuals. Capitalist enterprises, state agencies, political parties, football clubs, churches and tenants' associations are examples of actors in the minimal sense. They all have means of reaching decisions and of acting on at least some of them. Human individuals are distinctive in being the only actors whose actions do not always involve the actions of others. The actions of capitalist enterprises or community associations always depend on the actions of others – managers and other employees, elected officers, and sometimes other organizations. I call these 'social actors': each and every one of their actions depends on social relations with other actors.

I will return to the topic of social actors. For the moment, two words of warning are in order. One is that we should be wary of any suggestion that social actors can be discounted on the grounds that their actions are reducible to the actions of human individuals. Such reductionist claims rarely amount to more than a gesture and they do nothing to reduce the importance of analysing social actors and their conditions of action. Even if we were to accept in principle that social actors were always reducible to human individuals, we should still be concerned with investigating their decisions and actions and with their consequences. Secondly, the concept of actor is frequently extended to entities that have no identifiable means of reaching decisions, let alone of acting on them – for example, classes, societies, the human race. I argue that there are indeed actors other than human individuals, some of whom play an important part in the modern world, but that classes and societies are not among them.

Shortly after their comment on the behavioural rationality of mammals, Macdonald and Pettit go on argue to that beliefs and desires should be understood as propositional attitudes. These are

> states of mind which are identified most naturally by ref-
> erence to propositions that, in some sense, constitute their
> objects. Thus the belief that Paris is in France is a state of
> mind, conscious or unconscious, identified by reference to
> the proposition appearing in the that-clause, which tells us
> what in fact is believed: Paris is in France. A parallel story
> goes for desire. (ibid. p. 59)

There are two points to notice here. First, one respect in which humans differ from other animals, but not from social actors, is a consequence of their relation to language. Some of their decisions involve propositions which are formulated and which may (or may not) be spoken or written out. Secondly, the treatment of action as a function of 'states of mind', that is, of beliefs and desires, should not be allowed to pre-empt consideration both of what is to count as an actor and of the processes by which decisions are made. In conventional discussions of intentionality, propositional attitudes or states of mind are not attributed to capitalist enterprises and other social actors. Once the concept of actor is detached from that of the human individual, however, there is no reason to treat intentional action as the ontological privilege of human individuals. Decisions can then usefully be characterized in other terms. Here I argue that some decisions involve propositions that are formulated, some involve states of mind such as beliefs and desires, and some involve both.

Human individuals and social actors both make decisions that are formulated. Not all human decisions are of that kind. Some may not be conscious at all, and many will be habitual. Others are made on the basis of a practical knowledge that is not formulated at the moment of action. Driving techniques are a good example: once acquired the knowledge is rarely formulated and some of it will be difficult to formulate at all. But, while many human decisions are not formulated by the actor, decisions by other animals cannot be so formulated. There may well be a sense in which the ascription of belief and desire to the dog in the above example performs an explanatory role.[1] But there is no sense in which such propositional attitudes can be identified by reference to propositions that could be formulated by the dog, that is, by the actor in question. To say that some decisions are formulated by the actor is to say that the actor in question has the means of formulating those decisions. It is to raise questions of what means of formulating decisions (and other propositions) are available to that actor, and questions of the conditions on which they depend.

THE PORTFOLIO MODEL OF THE ACTOR

In his introduction to *Rational Choice* (1986) Elster describes rational choice explanation as a particular variety of intentional explanation. This last is 'characterized by various relations that obtain between, on the one hand, the action to be explained and, on the other hand, the desires and beliefs of the agent' (Elster, ed., 1986, p. 12). As he describes it, intentional explanation involves the assumptions of the minimal concept of actor together with the further assumption that an actor's decision is the rational product of states of mind that characterize that actor at the time of decision. Taken together these assumptions identify what I shall call the portfolio model of the actor. It treats action as resulting for the most part from intentions that are themselves the product of a portfolio of beliefs and desires which the actor carries around from one situation to another. Actors sort through their portfolios for the beliefs and desires that seem to be relevant to their situations and use them to identify possible courses of action and to choose between them. In this model the contents of the actor's portfolio may change from time to time, but at any given moment they are to be regarded as relatively stable.

Now, Elster's account of intentional explanation is entirely conventional; it presents the portfolio model as an unquestionable starting-point for intentional analysis. I introduced the minimal concept of actor above in order to show that the portfolio model is itself a refinement of something more general and abstract. One advantage of adopting the minimal concept of actor as starting-point for intentional analysis is that it requires us to recognize that not all intentions can be regarded as reflecting the states of mind of human individuals. It is only in the loosest sense that the decisions of social actors could be described as resulting from their beliefs, desires or other states of mind. The intentions of social actors raise important issues for social thought, concerning the conditions in which they are formed and the means by which they have their consequences. I return to that question in chapter 6, and in chapter 5 I argue that the portfolio model provides too limited an account of human action. For the moment, notice simply that intentional explanation need not depend on all the assumptions of the portfolio model. Rational choice analysis adopts the assumptions of the portfolio model and adds a few more.

My discussion of the portfolio model and its implications pays considerable attention to the work of Donald Davidson. This is partly because Elster, one of the more circumspect and philosophically aware of the many advocates of rational choice analysis, relies on Davidson's work in his own accounts of intentional explanation. The more important reason is that Davidson has provided one of the clearest and most sustained contemporary investigations of the character of intentional explanation. In particular, he offers a clear account of why the assumption of a 'large degree of rationality and consistency' (Davidson, 1980, p. 237) is such an important part of the portfolio model.[2] We shall see that rational choice analysis operates with a more restricted notion of rationality and a rather different account of its paradigmatic status.

Macdonald and Pettit present what I have called the portfolio model as if it were the 'everyday or orthodox conception of agents'. It is 'something which each of us picks up in developing competence at accounting for actions, both our own and those of other people'(1981, p. 58). Children do indeed pick up the strangest things, but in chapter 5 I argue that what 'each of us picks up' in that connection is something rather different. For the present we are concerned with the 'orthodox' conception of the agent, which Macdonald and Pettit describe as involving two distinct but related assumptions of rationality. First, there is the behavioural rationality of the minimal concept of actor, the assumption that action results from or expresses an intention. Secondly, there is attitudinal rationality, an assumption concerning relations between the actor's states of mind. We consider these assumptions in turn.

BEHAVIOURAL RATIONALITY

To explain an action as resulting from an actor's reasons is to say that there is a sense in which those reasons are a cause of the action. Many analytical philosophers have argued that reasons could not be causes on the grounds that the relation between an action and its reason is one that holds by virtue of their meanings. In other words, it is a 'logical' or 'internal' relation. There could be no such connection between a cause and its effects.[3] Davidson argued in 'Actions, reasons and causes' (in his 1980 volume) that whatever 'logical' connection may obtain between reason and action, it does not rule out a causal connection between them. These disputes will not be considered here, and for the purposes of this book I treat action as caused by the actor's reasons. Actors may also do things that are not caused in this way, but they would not be called actions.

To say that the actor's reasons explain an action is to say that they cause that action. It is not enough that they may be good reasons for the action, for good reasons might be *post hoc* rationalizations or excuses for behaviour caused in some other way. Or again, a 'man might have good reasons for killing his father, and yet the reasons not be his reasons in doing it (think of Oedipus)' (Davidson, 1980, p. 232). The reasons must also cause the behaviour in what Davidson calls 'the right way'. It is difficult to specify exactly what the right way is, but what it is not may be illustrated by examples. Think of Oedipus again:

> for suppose, contrary to the legend, that Oedipus, for some dark oedipal reason, was hurrying along the road, intent on killing his father, and, finding a surly old man blocking his way, killed him so he could (as he thought) get on with the main job. Then not only did Oedipus want to kill his father, and actually kill him, but his desire caused him to kill his father. Yet we could not say that in killing the old man he intentionally killed his father. (ibid.)

I will return to this example. For the moment notice that there is indeed a connection between Oedipus' intention to kill his father and the killing of the old man, but that it is indirect. It is only one of a number of elements that combine to provide him with a reason to kill the old man – who happens to be his father. In this case, the connection between the intention to kill his father and the act of killing him has itself to be explained. An intention causes action 'in the right way' if there is an immediacy or directness in the connection that is not there in Davidson's tale – that is, if no further explanation seems to be called for as to how the intention resulted in the action. The action 'expresses' its intention and there is a relation between them that Winch would call a 'logical' or 'internal' relation.

There are many respects in which this account of how reasons cause actions 'in the right way' remains obscure, but it will serve. Now consider a different respect in which the relation between reason and action may be problematic, the all too familiar phenomenon of weakness of will (also known as incontinence or akrasia) in which actors knowingly go against their own considered judgement. An example would be taking another drink before going home, having decided not to do so. Elster comments that 'the self-destructive behaviour which can arise when people act against their better judgement is so widespread in our societies that it ought to be given a

much more central place in the analysis of human action'
(Elster, ed., 1986, p. 16) than it receives in the literature of
rational choice.

Now, the difficulty that incontinence poses for the assumption
of behavioural rationality does not lie in the fact that actors sometimes behave irrationally. Behaviour does not always take the
form of action, and some of it may be without reason. In any
event, a limited amount of irrational behaviour need hardly conflict with the assumption that actors are by and large rational.
The trouble with incontinence is that in this case the actor does
have a reason for the action – and also what seemed to be a better
reason against it. The problem is then that 'the attempt to read
reason into the behaviour is necessarily subject to a degree of
frustration' (Davidson, 1980, p. 42). How can a person characterized by behavioural rationality perform an action having
decided, all things considered, that a different action would be
better? If reasons are causes, how is it possible that the best
of reasons is not always the most powerful of causes? (If reasons
were not thought to be causes, if their relation to action were
supposed to be an internal or logical one, then the problem of
incontinence would be even more of an embarrassment.)

The answer lies in an ambiguity in the notion of the comparative assessment of reasons. Possible reasons for action may
be compared in terms of their logical or internal relations with
the actor's beliefs and desires. I examine my reasons for having
one more drink before driving home and my reasons for not
having one in the light of my current portfolio of beliefs and
desires, and I decide that the second set of reasons is the
stronger. Then I have another drink. The reasons that are most
effective in this case are not the ones that seemed best in my
comparative judgement. Incontinence shows that the order of
internal relations amongst reasons does not always correspond
to the order of causal efficacy.

This result should not seem too surprising. In the case of
human actors, intentions can result in action only by means
of some physiological processes. My having the other drink
involves raising the glass to my mouth, swallowing, and a variety
of other movements as well. Action here appears to involve
two distinct orders of determination: first an order of beliefs,

desires and intentions, and secondly an order of physiological processes. (Action might also involve relations with other things, including other actors, but that complication has no bearing on the present issue.) Davidson insists, correctly in my view, that mental states just are brain states, so that the causal efficacy (such as it is) of an actor's reasons for action is a matter of their physiological characteristics.[4] It does not follow on this view that there is any unambiguous correspondence between analyses conducted at one level (in terms of internal relations between beliefs, desires and reasons) and those conducted at the other (in terms of physiology). For example, what would clearly count as instances of the same state of mind (wanting another drink) need not be instances of the same physiological conditions.

Reasons are causes by virtue of their physiological character, so that the order of internal or logical relations between ideas is not, strictly speaking, an order of determination at all. Readers who are unhappy with such thoroughgoing materialism must find some other way of coming to terms with the physiological character of human action. Consider, for example, the work of Talcott Parsons. In spite of its problems, it remains one of the most ambitious and theoretically sophisticated of sociological attempts to show how the physiological character of the human organism can be incorporated into social theory. He insists, in *Towards a General Theory of Action*, that 'the human organism has a constitutional capacity to react to objects, especially other human beings, without the specific content or form of the reaction being in any way physiologically given' (Parsons and Shils, 1962, p. 10).

On this view human action results from a combination of motivational-orientation, which provides the energy for action, and value-orientation, which provides its control. The energy for action is derived from the physiological organism through its gratification structure, and the direction or object of its action is given by its orientations. The personality system of the actor is dependent on its articulation with social and cultural systems on the one hand and the physiological organism on the other. This last means that the organization of beliefs, desires and the rest in the actor's personality is in part a function of a gratification structure relating to the actor's physiological sources of energy. Here, too, then physiological exigencies ensure that action does not always follow the order of internal relations between ideas.

In either case, then, the order of actors' meanings does not entirely correspond to the order of determination of their actions. If there were no correspondence at all, then the question of intentional analysis of actors' behaviour would not arise. To assume behavioural rationality is to assume that the two orders correspond reasonably well for much of the time.

Notice finally that while behavioural rationality has been discussed here in terms of human actors, analogous issues could be raised regarding the actions of social actors. I have used the case of incontinence to establish that there may be discrepancies between the order of meaningful relations between beliefs, desires and intentions on the one hand and the order of causal efficacy in the determination of action on the other. Discrepancies of another order are at stake in the actions of social actors: they depend on the intentions of human individuals and they depend on a more or less complex arrangement of social relations between actors. The policies of a local education authority (LEA) are translated into action through a number of different channels (advice and instructions to school heads, allocation of resources, regulation of teaching appointments and promotions, and so on). It may not be possible to account for what happens in the classroom without reference to the LEA's intentions, but what the LEA does to children and teachers cannot be treated simply as expressing its intentions more or less adequately. Similar considerations apply to other social actors.

ATTITUDINAL RATIONALITY

In the course of my discussion of incontinence I referred to the order of meaningful relations between beliefs, desires and intentions. The assumption of attitudinal rationality is an assumption about the character of that order. As part of their account of what they call the 'orthodox' conception of agents, Macdonald and Pettit present the core of attitudinal rationality in terms of a concern for the truth of propositions. If a set of propositions can be confronted with counter-examples or if it generates inconsistencies then it cannot be true. For an actor to be attitudinally rational 'is to be disposed at least to change one's beliefs so as to eliminate counter-examples and inconsistencies' (Macdonald and Pettit, 1981, p. 60). As for desires, they can be redescribed as evaluative beliefs: my desire for another drink translates into the belief that it is desirable that I have another drink. Accordingly, attitudinal rationality is a matter of there being a strain towards truth and consistency in the actor's portfolio of beliefs and desires. The portfolio, in other words, is assumed to be a relatively coherent whole.

Now, the portfolio model of the actor is normally introduced as the unquestionable starting-point for intentional analysis – so that behavioural and attitudinal rationality appear as different aspects of the one, more general rationality of the actor. According to Macdonald and Pettit, 'as we assume that an agent is behaviourally rational . . . so we assume at the same stroke that he possesses attitudinal rationality, being disposed to see that his beliefs are true' (ibid., p. 61). To see why behavioural and attitudinal rationality are thought to be related in this way is also to see why the assumption of rationality, in both aspects, is so often thought to be an essential part of intentional analysis.

The assumption of behavioural rationality tells us to treat action as resulting from some intention of the actor. When the actor is assumed to be a human individual this amounts to saying that it results from a state of mind. The action may then be explained by reference to the state of mind that produced it. How are those states of mind to be identified? The answer, of course, is that we have no alternative but to work back from the actor's behaviour (including verbal behaviour) by interpreting it as expressing the beliefs, desires and intentions that we wish to identify. To do so we have to assume that the behaviour in question results from states of mind – that it is indeed a matter of action, not an epileptic fit or a heart attack. We must also make some assumption about how the states of mind of the actor relate to each other. It is here that the assumption of attitudinal rationality is thought to be necessary to the understanding of actors as behaviourally rational.

To see what is at stake here consider the problems of understanding another culture. This has been an area of wide-ranging debate in anthropology and in philosophy, raising questions of the possibility of precise translation, the relativity of 'Western' rationality, and the like. Fortunately there are several excellent surveys of these debates, and their details need not concern us here.[5] I refer to the question of understanding another culture merely in order to bring out the general character of the assumption of attitudinal rationality. The problems of understanding appear in extreme form when it is a matter of getting to grips with an alien culture.

Suppose that you arrive in a remote and isolated society to find that you have no knowledge of its language and that there are few of the artefacts with which you are familiar from our culture. How do you set about understanding and making yourself understood? There are practical questions here that will be of little interest to most readers. More interesting for the present discussion is the question of what assumptions have to be made about the thought processes of these strangers in the course of attempting to come to terms with their language and way of life. With luck you learn pretty rapidly how to tell when food, drink and shelter are at issue.

Now suppose that while still at this early stage you find yourself suddenly surrounded by a crowd of these strangers. They appear to be agitated, and they may or may not be angry. (How can you tell?) Some of them point at you and seem to use words you recognize as something to do with food. To attempt any understanding of what is going on it is necessary to make some assumptions about their beliefs and desires. Are they cannibals? Have you been eating in a sacred place or at a time set aside for fasting? Are they competing with each other to exchange your jeans for yams, and bidding up the price as they do so?

The example is fanciful, but it will serve to illustrate a general point. If we wish to understand what people mean by what they say then we cannot do so without constructing some account of what they believe and what they desire. In Davidson's view 'the basic strategy must be to assume that by and large a speaker we do not yet understand is consistent and correct in his beliefs –

according to our own standards, of course' (Davidson, 1980, p. 238). This has been called the 'principle of charity' and, in a slightly different form, the 'principle of humanity.'[6] The suggestion is that not only is the assumption of rationality necessary for the practical purposes of inquiry, but that it is also desirable on the grounds that it frees the inquiry from the dangers of parochialism or ethnocentricity by attributing equal humanity to others, and especially to other peoples.[7]

Davidson proposes to extend the principle of charity from the analysis of what people say to the analysis of their behaviour generally. His argument is that to look for the intention behind an action is to seek to identify the beliefs and desires that led up to it.

> There is no assigning beliefs to a person one by one on the basis of his verbal behaviour, his choices, or other local signs no matter how plain and evident, for we make sense of particular beliefs only as they cohere with other beliefs, with preferences, with intentions, hopes, fears, expectations, and the rest. (ibid., p. 221)

Beliefs, desires and intentions are so interconnected in human behaviour that we cannot hope to analyse one without reference to the others. Davidson argues that we cannot make sense of their interconnections without also assuming rationality:

> if we are intelligibly to attribute attitudes and beliefs, or usefully to describe motions as behaviour, then we are committed to finding, in the pattern of behaviour, belief and desire, a large degree of rationality and consistency. (ibid., p. 237)

This is an holistic conception of rationality. It applies not only to individual items of behaviour but also to the actor's behaviour as a whole.

I have presented this issue in Davidson's terms because his work provides a particularly clear example of what is involved in the widely held view that the presumption of a fair degree of rationality is necessary to the task of understanding the behaviour of others. Davidson insists that the 'rationality' that we assume here must be understood according to our own standards. What of the argument that the understanding of other cultures requires precisely that we do not impose Western norms of rationality, and that the principle of charity is a kind of 'linguistic imperialism' (Hacking, 1975, p. 149)?[8] Consider Winch's commentary on Evans-Pritchard's *Witchcraft, Oracles and Magic among the Azande*. Evans-Pritchard was firmly convinced of the falsity of Zande beliefs regarding witchcraft and the poison oracle. He describes his own occasional reaction 'to misfortune in the idiom of witchcraft' as if it were a 'lapse into unreason' (1976, p. 45).

Winch disputes the presumption that Zande beliefs and practices were irrational; 'if *our* concept of rationality is a different one from his, then it makes no sense to say that anything either does or does not appear rational to *him* in *our* sense' (Winch, 1970, p. 97). This seems to be a relativistic conception of rationality. Nevertheless, as Macdonald and Pettit argue, there remains a sense in which Winch's position accords with the principle of humanity. Institutionalized science is not a characteristic of Azande culture, so that individual Zande cannot assess magic in the same way as would denizens of Western societies. What has to be explained, then, is not why individual Zande are irrational in their attachment to magic, oracles and the like, but rather why the social institutions of scientific practice have not appeared in their society.

We can therefore understand Winch's position not so much as a rejection of cross-cultural comparison, but rather as a critique of a specific mode of comparison that identifies rationality with the acceptance of the norms and findings of modern science. In societies that are unfamiliar with modern science that view of rationality is clearly inappropriate. Winch remains committed to the presumption of rationality, understood in a more general sense:

> To say of a society that it has language is also to say that it
> has a concept of rationality. There need not perhaps be any
> word functioning in its language as 'rational' does in ours,
> but at least there must be features of its members' use of

language analogous to those features of our use of language which are connected with our use of the word 'rational'. (ibid., p. 99)

This returns us to the general argument. The assumption that action results from intention commits us to a 'hermeneutic' process of understanding the behaviour of others, and that process in turn requires us to make the further holistic assumption of rationality.

In effect, the portfolio model presents us with a view of behaviour as resulting from intentions which are themselves the product of a portfolio of beliefs and desires. The content of the portfolio may change from time to time but at any given time it is assumed to be relatively stable. Actors carry their portfolios around from situation to situation and use them as the starting-point for rational deliberation about possible courses of action. Given that account of the actor, intentional analysis requires that we work back to actors' beliefs and desires by constructing an interpretation of their behaviour, including, of course, an interpretation of what they say. The process of constructing an account of an actor's beliefs and desires from observation of behaviour in various contexts requires us to presume a fair degree of rationality and consistency. It stands to reason, so to speak, that we could not otherwise hope to work back from some pattern of behaviour to infer the beliefs and desires that have produced it.

I argue in chapter 5 that the particular beliefs and desires and the large degree of rationality and consistency that we must, on this account, attribute to actors are all artefacts of the portfolio model of the actor. Similarly for our attempts at translation. The requirement that we must assume consistency 'according to our own standards' if we are to grasp what is meant by a speaker we do not yet understand, is itself an artefact of a portfolio model of verbal behaviour.

Once again, I have discussed the issue of attitudinal rationality in terms of human actors. Here too it is instructive to consider how that issue appears in the case of social actors. We are concerned, say, with the pattern of investment displayed by a large corporation, and we try to understand that behaviour as resulting from a mixture of standing policies and recent decisions. Intentional analysis in this case is hardly going to lead us in the direction of interpreting those policies as resulting from the consistent application of some more or less stable portfolio of beliefs and desires. Decisions are made and policies laid down at a variety of points within the organization, and we are more likely to interpret them in terms of the application of particular accounting practices, institutionalized techniques of information-gathering and assessment, decision-making procedures, and their relationships to decisions and policies emanating from elsewhere.[9] There is certainly no reason in general to suppose that policies and decisions reflect some overall 'rationality' that is characteristic of the actor *qua* actor.

Apart from its intrinsic importance, consideration of the actions of social actors has the advantage that it undermines the apparent obviousness of the assumptions of the portfolio model. Why should we assume an holistic model of the actor, characterized by an overall intrinsic rationality, in interpreting the decisions of some kinds of actor, and look for the particular techniques and practices employed in reaching decisions through a variety of dispersed decision-making processes in the case of others? The presumption of a holistic rationality is not a necessary ingredient of the concept of actor.

RATIONAL CHOICE AND THE PORTFOLIO MODEL

The portfolio model involves a considerable refinement of the minimal concept of the actor but it remains relatively formal and abstract. If we assume that actors are also human individuals then it is tempting to build what we believe to be other features of human individuals into our basic concept of actor. For example, after presenting the *core* of attitudinal rationality as a disposition to worry about the truth and consistency of one's beliefs, Macdonald and Pettit then go on to say that this

> is not the entire substance. To be responsive to counter-examples and inconsistencies might be more or less to stand still, forever improving the profile of a given stock

of beliefs. In fact human beings are inevitably involved in the continuous extension and adaptation of their beliefs. (Macdonald and Pettit, 1981, p. 60)

I argue in chapter 5 that the further assumptions involved here tend to undermine the integrity of the portfolio model. For the moment, notice that the claim that there are actors other than human individuals requires a rigorous separation between the analysis of action in general and the analysis of human action in particular. Action is always performed by some particular actor, and the characteristics of that actor will be relevant to an investigation of its actions. But how precisely they are relevant can be understood only if we first distinguish clearly between our concept of action and those characteristics.

Rational choice analysis modifies the portfolio model in a different way by adding a further, utilitarian constraint to the assumption of attitudinal rationality. In its simplest form this involves the assumption outlined in chapter 3 that the desires in the actor's portfolio are ordered by a preference ranking that is both transitive and complete. It is widely recognized, of course, that this basic utilitarian model gives a relatively unsophisticated account of human behaviour. For some purposes rational choice analysis admits that it may be necessary to introduce further refinements of their basic model, and perhaps to recognize the intervention of non-rational elements in behaviour. Numerous possibilities have been explored in the literature and I gave several examples in chapter 2. The claim of rational choice analysis is not that action is always rational, quite the contrary, but rather that its model of rational action should have a paradigmatic status for explanation in the social sciences. I have already quoted, for example, Hardin's assertion that 'the assumption of narrowly rational motivation yields predictions that are the most useful benchmark by which to assess the extent and the impact of other motivations' (Hardin, 1982, p. 11)

Of course it yields predictions. The question is: why should those predictions be taken as a benchmark for further inquiry? There are two issues here. First, there is nothing in the argument that we are committed to finding a large degree of rationality and consistency in actors' behaviour that requires us also to find them employing for the most part some version of the utilitarian calculus.

The second issue is less straightforward. It concerns not so much the content of the assumption of rationality, but rather the character of the paradigmatic status that is claimed for it. It is one thing to argue, with Davidson, that the presumption of rationality is necessary if we are to be able to unravel the beliefs and desires of actors; and further, that only when we can do that will we be in a position to identify instances of non-rational behaviour. It is quite another to insist that a general presumption of rationality must be used as a benchmark in the investigation of any behaviour that we might wish to explain.

To see what is at stake here notice that the question of explanation rarely arises with regard to the full generality of the behaviour of some actor or actors. We are not concerned with everything they do but rather with accounting for some particular course of action or pattern of behaviour. The general presumption of the principle of charity, that the actors concerned are 'by and large' rational, tells us nothing about the motivations involved in the particular actions we wish to explain. 'But nothing can explain an agent's (intentional) actions except something that motivates him so to act' (Williams, 1979, p. 22). What has to be investigated here is what Williams calls the subjective motivational set of the actor or actors in question, involving such things as 'dispositions of evaluation, patterns of emotional reaction, personal loyalties, and various projects . . . embodying commitments of the agent'(ibid., p. 20).

Now, the claim of rational choice analysis that the assumption of rationality should have a paradigmatic status implies a different kind of investigation. Rather than inquire into the subjective motivational set of the actors concerned, it asks us to investigate what would motivate rational actors to perform the actions that are to be explained. Those motivations then constitute our benchmark for investigating the impact of other motivations.

Hardin's comments on voting behaviour, quoted at the beginning of chapter 2, are to be understood in this spirit. The assumption of narrowly rational motivations provides a poor explanation precisely because it implies that 'almost no one would voluntarily vote in, say, American national elections. It helps us to understand why half of eligible Americans do not vote, but it does little to help us understand the other half' (Hardin, 1982, p. 11). In other words, we understand those who do not vote, not in terms of some investigation of their own motivations, but rather in terms of the hypothetical motivations of idealized rational actors. At the end of chapter 2 I noted something similar in Przeworski's examination of the development of socialist movements in Western Europe. Rather than an historical investigation of the objectives and the forms of political calculation employed in these movements, he provides an explanation in terms of what rational actors would have done in their circumstances.

To conclude this section consider two rather different examples, both involving decisions with wide-ranging social consequences. In each case the benchmark of rationality would require that we invoke non-rational elements only when all attempts at constructing an explanation of the decisions as rational finally break down. The first example concerns the British coal crisis in the winter of 1946–7. Severe weather combined with a series of incompetent ministerial decisions led to prolonged cuts in power supplies and a substantial loss of industrial production.

> It was a striking example of incompetence in economic planning by a government dedicated to economic planning. What stood revealed was not the limitations on which the text-books insist – the problems of decentralizing and yet achieving coordination, the uncertainties and lack of adequate information. On the contrary, the uncertainties were minimal, the information abundant, the organization impressive. The lesson was rather that planning depends on planners, that when ministers plan they may have no sense of magnitudes and dismiss statistical analysis with an airy reference to 'imponderables'. (Cairncross, 1985, p. 383)

The principle of charity requires us to assume that Shinwell, the minister primarily responsible for the unnecessarily large scale of the crisis, was by and large rational and consistent in the conduct of his affairs. But that is no reason to seek to fabricate an explanation for his action in this particular case as if it were rational.

Now consider Sen's comment on the disastrous impact of misleading and simplistic models of economic life in poor societies on policies for famine relief.

> If one person in eight starves regularly in the world, this [should be] seen as the result of his inability to establish entitlement to enough food; the question of the physical availability of food is not directly involved . . . The mesmerizing simplicity of focusing on the ratio of food to population has persistently played an obscuring role over centuries, and continues to plague policy discussions today much as it has deranged anti-famine policies in the past. (Sen, 1981, p. 8)

Briefly, the argument is that relief agencies have too often seen their task primarily as one of getting supplies to the affected area, on the assumption that this is what they do best. One further assumption here is that existing channels of distribution would be the most acceptable and efficient means of giving the food out to the famine-stricken population. What happens is that most of those in the greatest need, from the point of view of the relief agencies, are last in line when it comes to distribution of supplies. The reason is simple: they are most in need precisely because they are last in line according to existing channels of distribution.

Why have so many relief efforts failed to take account of the character of distribution relations and entitlements in the communities they were trying to help? Here, too, it may well be that the policy-makers and administrators were 'by and large' rational in the conduct of their lives – but that is hardly the point. We are not concerned with how they conduct their lives overall, but with accounting for the persistence of an irrational concentration on the physical availability of food and a corresponding neglect of the place of food in the pattern of exchange entitlements throughout the society.

This brings me to my final comment. The disastrous decisions in this example seem to be the result not so much of the beliefs and desires of policy-makers and administrators as of a particular way of thinking about the problem. How do 'ways of thinking' fit into rational choice analysis and the more general portfolio model? I take up this question in the following chapter.

5

Rationality, action and deliberation

I have suggested that rational choice analysis takes up a more general model of the rationality of intentional behaviour and modifies it in two important respects. First, it treats the preferences and desires of the actor as exhibiting a utilitarian structure, and secondly it assigns a distinctive kind of paradigmatic status to the assumption of rationality. There is nothing in the assumption that intentional action is by and large rational to justify either modification. This chapter argues that there are serious problems with that more general model of intentional action and suggests that it obscures important questions of the techniques, procedures and forms of thought employed by actors in the course of their behaviour.

The more general model of intentional behaviour is based on what I have called the portfolio model of the actor. Action results from the application of a more or less stable portfolio of beliefs and desires to the situation of action. The actor sorts through the portfolio for those beliefs and desires that seem to have a bearing on the situation and uses them to decide what to do. We saw in chapter 4 that this model brings together two rather different senses in which actors are supposed to be rational. First there is behavioural rationality, the assumption that action results from or expresses that actor's intentions. Secondly there is what Macdonald and Pettit call attitudinal rationality, the assumption of a strain towards truth and consistency in the actor's portfolio of beliefs and desires. We have seen that behavioural and attitudinal rationality are generally regarded as different aspects of the one overall rationality of the actor, as if to assume the first is also necessarily to assume the second. In effect, the portfolio model presents an holistic conception of the actor's rationality. Rationality is supposed to be exhibited in the actor's overall pattern of behaviour, not merely in particular items of behaviour. This chapter disputes that holistic conception of actors' rationality.

Now, I have deliberately presented the portfolio model as a refinement of a still more general model of the actor, based simply on the assumption of behavioural rationality. Action results from the actor's intentions, and an actor is anything that is able to form intentions and to act on them. Human individuals and social actors of various kinds are all actors in this minimal sense and so, on some interpretations of intention, are many other animals. Questions of attitudinal rationality arise in relation to beliefs and desires that can be understood as propositional attitudes. This means that they may not always arise in the case of human action and that they do not arise at all in the case of non-human animals.

As for social actors, I have noted two reasons why we should not assume attitudinal rationality. First, state agencies, capitalist enterprises and political parties are indeed actors in the minimal sense that some of what they do is based on decisions. But there is something distinctly odd about an interpretation of the decisions of these and other social actors as resulting from their beliefs, desires and other states of mind. Secondly, the decisions of many social actors are made at various points within the organization and are reached through a variety of decision-making processes. There is no reason here to suppose that those decisions reflect an holistic rationality that is characteristic of the actor *qua* actor.

Consideration of social actors and non-human animals undermines the apparent obviousness of the portfolio model of the actor. There is room for debate about the senses in which cats or koalas can be said to form intentions and act on them and I shall not pursue that issue here.[1] Social actors on the other hand clearly do act on the basis of decisions that are formulated. Although they do not have propositional attitudes, in the sense of beliefs, desires and other states of mind, their actions nevertheless result from intentions in the form of propositions. The intentions of both human individuals and social actors sometimes involve propositions. Why should we assume an holistic rationality in the case of one category of actor and not in the other?

This chapter disputes the assumption of an holistic rationality even in the case of human actors. Now, we have seen that Davidson and others advance a powerful argument to the effect that once we assume that a (human) actor is behaviourally rational we must also assume that the actor possesses attitudinal rationality. The assumption that action results from intentions commits us to a process of understanding actors' beliefs and desires by working back from their behaviour, including, of course, their verbal behaviour. We can do that, Davidson argues, only if we assume that there is 'in the pattern of behaviour, belief and desire, a large degree of rationality and consistency' (Davidson, 1980, p. 237). To show that the assumption of an holistic rationality is mistaken it will be necessary to counter that argument.

The trouble with describing action as the rational product of actors' beliefs and desires is that it says nothing about those processes of evaluation, calculation and reflection that sometimes play an important part in actors' choices between alternative courses of action. On the assumption of an holistic rationality there is no problem here. The actor selects those beliefs and desires that have a bearing on the choice to be made and deploys them in a rational assessment of the alternatives. In effect, the portfolio model allows that there may be some process of assessment involved in the formation of the actor's intention and proceeds to treat it as a transparent intermediary between beliefs and desires on the one hand and the action resulting from them on the other. The process is transparent because it takes the form of a rational deduction leading from premises, the relevant beliefs and desires, to their conclusion, the actor's intention. This type of connection between belief, desire and intention is exhibited by rational actors simply by virtue of their rationality. What more is there to say?

I argue that the problem with treating action as resulting from belief and desire is not that it denies the existence of processses of assessment but that it takes their rationality for granted. The 'large degree of rationality and consistency' Davidson requires us to find follows from that assumption. In that respect it is an artefact of a feature of the portfolio model of the actor that I have not so far brought into question. Once some definite process of thought is admitted as an element in our account of an actor's decision, then that process may be regarded as an object of investigation. I begin by considering two influential ways in which the transparent rationality of that process has been questioned. One concerns the notion of satisficing or bounded rationality, and the other involves the claim that there may be distinct rationalities or styles of reasoning. I conclude this chapter by questioning the role of beliefs and desires in the explanation of behaviour.

BOUNDED RATIONALITY

In the literature on rational choice perhaps the best-known alternative to the assumption of perfect rationality is Simon's concept of bounded rationality.[2] Where the assumption of perfect rationality locates all constraints in the actor's external environment Simon argues that there are important constraints arising from limitations of the actor, considered as an information processor. Actors are subject to bounded rationality in the sense that they are frequently unable to take account of all the available information, compile exhaustive lists of alternative courses of action, and ascertain the value and probability of each of the possible outcomes.

Simon insists that the source of the difficulty does not lie solely in the complexity of the outside world. That complexity poses a problem only because actors are limited in their cognitive capacities. Whilst it may not pose a problem for the God of Christian theology, other actors have no choice but to act within their cognitive limitations. In Simon's view this means that they 'satisfice' rather than maximize. They economize on the collection of information and evaluation of alternatives by searching only for a course of action that achieves a satisfactory result. What they aspire to, in other words, is something above an acceptable minimum, and what that is may change with new information or their discovery of new techniques. But it is not the maximum of perfect rationality.

Actors satisfice by adopting habits and operating rules to simplify calculation and the search for information in situations that are likely to be repeated, and they adopt general principles of action which can be expected to yield satisfactory results in the long run. For example, I brush my teeth every morning but I do not normally calculate whether it is in my best interests to do so. Capitalist enterprises seek what they regard as satisfactory levels of profit and other measures of performance, they resort to feedback rather than attempt to forecast all future conditions, and they use standard operating procedures and rules of thumb to make and implement many decisions. Or again, studies of voting behaviour regularly show that many voters are extremely ill-informed about politics. They recognize the names of few senior politicians, are ignorant of the policy positions of the party they support, and so on. Voting under conditions of such ignorance is clearly not perfectly rational but it could be interpreted as a kind of satisficing behaviour. Indeed, Downs (1957) argues that ignorance on the part of voters may well be rational in view of the limited effect of any one person's vote and the costs of obtaining information. Rational voters will rely on easily recognizable cues, slogans and party labels in making their decisions.

Simon's actors are rational beings, but finite. Satisficing behaviour is their rational response to the recognition of finitude. The finitude of actors is undeniable, but what of the other side of Simon's account, namely their rationality? Bounded rationality looks like a kind of rationality and Simon certainly presents it as such. However, the sense of 'rationality' involved here is hardly a robust one. Some commentators have interpreted satisficing as maximizing behaviour that takes account of information costs – rather along the lines of Downs' treatment of voters' ignorance (Riker and Ordershook, 1973). This is misleading: if we have no alternative but to satisfice in deciding on courses of action, how do we decide what forms of assessment to employ in making those decisions? If we cannot process all the information required in per-fectly rational decision-making how can we possibly make a perfectly rational evaluation of the forms of assessment available to us?[3]

The answer, of course, is that we must satisfice. We choose the techniques we employ in making our satisficing decisions according to some standards of satisfactory performance and we choose those standards in the same way. Bounded rationality, then, is a matter of actors doing the best they can according to standards which seem to them to be appropriate. What those standards are in any particular case should be a matter for investigation. There is no good reason to assume that they will always be standards of what an observer would regard as rationality.

STYLES OF REASONING

This last point brings us to a second issue. Where the notion of bounded rationality suggests that actors are less than fully rational because they are finite we must now consider the suggestion that they may employ different ways of thinking. There is an enormous literature on this issue with contributions from anthropology, philosophy, the history of the sciences, and other areas. Winch (1958, 1970) uses Evans-Pritchard's *Witchcraft, Oracles and Magic among the Azande* to suggest what seems to be a relativistic conception of rationality. Kuhn (1970) and Feyerabend (1975, 1978) have argued that the sciences have developed through distinct systems of thought that are mutually incommensurable. Quine has suggested that there is an indeterminacy of translation between the languages of truly disparate communities. Foucault[4] has explored a number of fundamental transformations in the organization of theoretical and practical knowledges of European societies. Many other examples could be cited.

There can be no question here of attempting a survey of these various arguments and the objections that have been brought against them. Instead, I propose to use Hacking's notion of 'styles of reasoning' to dispose of the assumption of an holistic rationality. Hacking (1982) develops his argument in the context of the history of the sciences and I shall adapt it to a more general purpose. The idea that there are radically different ways of thinking has generally been put forward in terms of a distinction between conceptual scheme and reality, and Davidson has put forward a powerful and effective critique of that distinction. On Davidson's account the idea of distinct conceptual schemes has no sense, and there is therefore no question of conceptual relativity. After briefly presenting Hacking's 'styles of reasoning' I consider Davidson's critique of the dualism of scheme and reality. In fact the notion of styles of reasoning does not involve that dualism and it implies a different kind of relativity to the one that Davidson rejects. Finally, I consider the relevance of styles of reasoning for more general questions of intentional analysis.

The idea that there are different ways of thinking is a commonplace in the history of the sciences. Consider just two of the many examples Hacking cites of outmoded styles of thought. One concerns the doctrines of resemblance and similitude of Renaissance medicine, alchemy and astrology. The problem we find with these doctrines is not so much that they are incommensurable with our modern sciences as that they advance propositions and defend them in ways that are entirely alien to us. It is possible to learn hermetic lore, but what would be learned is not simply how to translate from their language to ours, but rather the style of reasoning they employed. 'What we have to learn is not what they took for true, but what they took for true-or-false. (For example, that mercury salve might be good for syphilis because mercury is signed by the planet Mercury which signs the marketplace, where syphilis is contracted.)' (Hacking, 1982, p. 60)

The other example is closer to home:

At the time of Laplace it was very sensible to think that there are particles of caloric, the substance of heat, that have repulsive forces that decay rapidly with distance. On such an hypothesis Laplace solved many of the outstanding problems about sound. Propositions about the rate of extinction of the repulsive force of caloric were up for grabs as true or false and one knew how to obtain information bearing on the question. Laplace had an excellent estimate of the rate of extinction of the repulsive force, yet it turns out that the whole idea is wrongheaded. (ibid., pp. 55–6)

There is no difficulty about translating Laplace's arguments into the idiom of modern science. An assumption that turned out to be false sustained what was once a highly respectable style of scientific reasoning.

What distinguishes styles of reasoning in Hacking's account is not so much what they hold to be true, but rather what propositions become candidates for being true or false. The hermetic style of reasoning generates candidates for truth or falsity in one way, and the theory of caloric in another. In both cases, many of their candidates for truth or falsity would not now be considered as candidates at all. Hacking argues that there is an important difference between 'those propositions that have a sense for almost all human beings regardless of reasoning, and those that get a sense only within a style of reasoning' (ibid., p. 57).

THE DUALISM OF SCHEME AND REALITY

A familiar but misleading way of looking at differences in ways of thinking makes use of a distinction between conceptual scheme and reality: different conceptual schemes involve different ways of thinking about the world. To see why the distinction is misleading consider two rather different uses of the idea. In the history of the sciences it can be found in the concepts of paradigm and incommensurability proposed by Kuhn and, in a more radical form, by Feyerabend. These concepts have been subject to a variety of competing interpretations, but the underlying notion is clear enough. The suggestion is that there are different systems of thought in the history of the sciences which are incommensurable in the literal sense that they do not share a common measure. They address distinct sets of problems using distinct sets of concepts. Even when what might seem to be the same concepts are at stake (mercury or syphilis in hermetic and modern medicine) those concepts derive their meaning from the paradigms to which they belong.

On this view, the history of the sciences is the history of movement through a series of distinct conceptual schemes, each presenting a rather different reality. During the period of transition, of course, there will be some 'overlap between the problems that can be solved by the old and the new paradigm. But there will also be a decisive difference in the modes of solution. When the transition is complete, the profession will have changed its view of the field, its methods, and its goals' (Kuhn, 1970, pp. 84–5). In a famous comment on the nature of that transition Kuhn compares it to a change in visual *Gestalt* and proceeds to suggest that the 'parallel can be misleading. Scientists do not see something as something else; instead they simply see it ... In addition, the scientist does not preserve the gestalt subject's freedom to switch back and forth between ways of seeing' (ibid., p. 85)

The important point to notice for present purposes is how the concepts of paradigm and incommensurability depend on a distinction between conceptual scheme and reality. Distinct paradigms involve distinct conceptual schemes which present their adherents with distinct realities, or distinct perceptions of the same reality. It is because they present distinct perceptions that the paradigms are incommensurable. They do not present alternative accounts of the same phenomena, but rather different phenomena and accounts of them. They do not share a common set of perceptions which would allow scientists to choose between one paradigm and the other. Kuhn and Feyerabend stress incommensurability in order to combat the popular (Popperian) misconception that scientific development is primarily a matter of scientists choosing between increasingly successful theories by testing one against the other. The argument is not that adherents of different paradigms cannot dispute with each other. Quite the contrary. The point is that there will be disputes between them that cannot all be settled by an appeal to the facts.

A rather different use of the distinction between scheme and reality is Quine's thesis of the indeterminacy of translation. Quine defines a conceptual scheme as a set of sentences held to be true. Sentences at the core of a scheme are unlikely to be relinquished in the light of argument or evidence. They are protected from refutation by a periphery of sentences which are treated as empirical and which may be given up in the light of experience. If different languages involve different schemes how do native speakers of those languages ever communicate? Quine's argument is not, of course, that no translation is possible. Where human communities have been in contact and survived the experience they have always managed to establish communication about a variety of mundane issues. The point rather is that there can be no way of establishing a definitively correct method of translation from one language to the other. This means that no method of translation will turn out to be entirely satisfactory. To say that there is an indeterminacy of translation is to say that there are infinitely many different possible translations between the languages of disparate communities.

Although they lead in different directions the theses of incommensurability and the indeterminacy of translation share a common foundation in what Davidson calls 'the dogma of the dualism of scheme and reality' (Davidson, 1984, p. 198). If there are indeed distinct conceptual schemes of the kind Quine describes then there can be no common ground of perceptions, of sentences held to be true, that would allow us to choose between them. If there are infinitely many possible translations then there is none that is definitively correct, and no possibility therefore of testing propositions of one scheme against the reality described by the other. On the other hand, if there are incommensurable paradigms then there can be no satisfactory method of translating propositions from one to the other, only a variety of more or less unsatisfactory translations. The dualism of scheme and reality seems to lead inexorably in the direction of a conceptual relativity.

Davidson's paper 'On the very idea of a conceptual scheme' (in Davidson, 1984) cuts the ground from under incommensurability and the indeterminacy of translation by disposing of the dualism of scheme and reality on which they both depend. The dualism of scheme and reality associates having a conceptual scheme with having a language. Speakers of different languages may share a conceptual scheme, but only if one language can be translated into the other. To say that there are distinct conceptual schemes is to say that there are languages without translation between them. We can distinguish two possible claims: one that there is total failure of translation between schemes, and the other that there is only partial failure.

Davidson counters the first by arguing that there is no criterion for something to be a language (or a conceptual scheme) that does not also suppose it to be interpretable. His argument is that the attempt to characterize languages or conceptual schemes in some other way, for example, in terms of a common stock of meanings or of fitting raw experience, the facts, or whatever, comes down to the idea that something may be a conceptual scheme only if it is largely true. The criterion of a conceptual scheme radically different from our own then becomes 'largely true but not translatable' (ibid., p. 194). The final step is then to argue that there is not much sense to be made of a notion of truth, as applied to another language, independent of the possibility of translation.

We are left then with the second possibility, the claim that there is some common ground between schemes and only partial failure of translation between them. The common ground allows us to identify areas where translation breaks down. Davidson's argument here returns us to the principle of charity which I considered in chapter 4. If we are to establish that there is indeed a failure of translation rather than a difference of belief or opinion we must be able to identify what sentences are held to be true by speakers of the other language. To do that, in Davidson's view, we must adopt the principle of charity. 'Until we have successfully established a systematic correlation of sentences held true with sentences held true, there are no mistakes to make. Charity is forced on us; whether we like it or not, if we want to understand others we must count them right on most matters' (ibid., p. 197).

Where does the principle of charity leave the case for conceptual relativism?

> The answer is, I think, that we must say the same thing about differences in conceptual scheme as we say about differences in belief: we improve the clarity and bite of declarations of difference ... by enlarging the basis of shared (translatable)

language or of shared opinion. Indeed, no clear line between the cases can be made out ... when others think differently from us, no general principle, or appeal to evidence, can force us to decide that the difference lies in our beliefs rather than in our concepts. (ibid.)

Davidson therefore concludes that conceptual relativism has no solid meaning. Given the principle of charity 'we could not be in a position to judge that others had concepts or beliefs radically different from our own' (ibid.). The argument is not that communication is possible between people who have different schemes, for Davidson can find no sense in which it could be said that schemes are different.

Given the dogma of a dualism of scheme and reality, we get conceptual relativity, and truth relative to a scheme. Without the dogma, this kind of relativity goes by the board. (ibid., p. 198)

ANOTHER KIND OF RELATIVITY

I suggested earlier that the problem with treating action as resulting from belief and desire is that it pays no attention to the processes of calculation, evaluation or reflection that sometimes play an important part in actors' choices between courses of action. There is a related problem in Davidson's critique of conceptual relativity. A crucial step in his argument turns on the principle of charity. This involves the claim that we cannot identify an actor's concepts without at the same time constructing an account of the same actor's beliefs and desires; and in order to do that we have to interpret in a way that maximizes agreement. If only beliefs, concepts and desires were all we had to deal with then the argument would be difficult to dispute. What is missing, in Hacking's view, is any recognition of the distinction between statements which require no style of reasoning and statements whose sense depends on a particular style of reasoning. 'Davidson writes as if all sentences were of the former class. I agree that "my skin is warm" is of that class' (Hacking, 1982, p. 62).

'My skin is warm' is an appropriate example, both because Davidson uses it (1984, p. 194) and because Hacking finds it (or rather 'my skin is warmed') in Herschel's investigations of the theory of radiant heat. In the course of his investigations Herschel proposed and later rejected the following sentence. 'The heat which has the refrangibility of the red rays is occasioned by the light of those rays' (cited in Hacking, 1982, p. 63). The problem this poses for a sufficiently foreign translator is not primarily that the words 'ray' and 'refrangibility' are theoretical terms whose meaning depends on some definite paradigm. The problem rather 'is that the sufficiently foreign person will not have Herschel's kind of sentence as the sort of thing that can be true-or-false, because the ways of reasoning that bear on it are unknown. To exaggerate the case, say that the translator is Archimedes. I do not choose him at random, for he wrote a great tract on burning mirrors and was a greater scientist than Herschel. Yet I say he would not be able to effect a translation until he had caught up with some scientific method' (ibid.).

Hacking's argument here does not concern 'those boring domains of "observations" that we share with all people as people' (ibid., p. 61).The claim is that 'for part of our language, and perhaps as part of any language, being true or false is a property of sentences only because we reason about those sentences in certain ways' (ibid., p. 64). For many sentences, then, their status as possible candidates for truth or falsity is relative to styles of reasoning. The point about Herschel's sentence quoted above is not that he held it to be true. At one time he did and at another he did not, but in both cases the sentence was one whose truth was open to investigation. Similarly for the possible connection between mercury and syphilis in the hermetic tradition of medicine. It was possible to disagree about that connection within the hermetic tradition while regarding it as a viable case for investigation.

Styles of reasoning differ according to what may be candidates for truth or falsity and how they may be investigated. They do not confront reality in the ways that conceptual schemes or paradigms are supposed to confront reality.They do not present us with different perceptions of the world, but rather with different ways of proposing, investigating and arguing about propositions. Nor do styles of reasoning correspond to Quine's conceptual schemes, which are sets of sentences held to be true. In Quine's discussion the problem of indeterminacy of translation arises from the idea of a truth-preserving algorithm for matching sentences in the two languages. In fact, Hacking argues 'the possibilities available in one language are not there in the other. To get them into the second language one has to learn a way of reasoning and when that has been done there is no problem of translation at all, let alone indeterminacy' (ibid., p. 61).

Since the idea of 'style of reasoning' does not depend on 'the dogma of a dualism of scheme and reality' (Davidson, 1984, p. 198) it does not fall within Davidson's critique. Davidson's argument disposes very effectively of one kind of conceptual relativism, but it leaves room for another. 'The relativist ought to say that there might be whole other categories of truth-or-falsehood than ours' (Hacking, 1982, p. 64). Sometimes these categories are within easy reach of our own, as in Laplace's investigations of the rate of diminution of the repulsive force of caloric. Sometimes they are considerably more remote. In the latter case 'the rationality of a style of reasoning as a way of bearing on the truth of a class of propositions does not seem open for independent criticism, because the very sense of what can be established by that style depends upon the style itself' (ibid., p. 56).

ACTION AND DELIBERATION

What has all this to do with the portfolio model of the actor? If action results from the beliefs and desires of the actor then it is difficult to avoid the conclusion that we have to assume something like Davidson's principle of charity if we wish to understand the actions of others. We must assume, in other words, that others are broadly correct in their beliefs and that by and large they are rational, in our sense of rationality. Once we recognize that action sometimes results from actors' deliberations things look rather different. Simon uses the notion of bounded rationality to argue that the limited cognitive capacities of actors imply that their decisions are often less than fully rational. Actors satisfice by making decisions involving deliberate simplifications, economizing on information gathering and processing, and so on. They do so according to standards of adequacy rather than of perfect rationality, and the standards they employ are themselves the result of satisficing.

At first sight there seems little difficulty about accommodating the idea of bounded rationality to Davidson's principle of charity. The claim that actors are less than fully rational because they are finite is entirely compatible with the claim that they are by and large rational. The difficulty lies in the 'rationality' of bounded rationality. Since Simon's actors have limited cognitive capacities there is no reason to suppose that they can identify the most rational form of satisficing for their purposes. The implication here is that actors may satisfice in a variety of ways, making different simplifications, economizing on information-gathering and processing by adopting different rules of thumb, and choosing to accept different standards of adequacy in the decision-making procedures they adopt. The analysis of action in terms of actors' choices therefore requires investigation of the decision-making procedures employed by the actors in question rather than any blanket assumption that they are all rational in much the same way. The significance of Simon's argument for the portfolio model does not lie in the claim that rationality is bounded. Rather it lies in his insistence on the importance of actors' deliberations for at least some of their actions.

Where bounded rationality suggests that actors' deliberations are often less than fully rational Hacking proposes that there are distinct rationalities or styles of reasoning. Hacking develops the argument in the context of the history of the sciences, but it has more general implications. Much of what scientists have to say cannot be understood without reference to the style of reasoning they employ. In other words, scientific claims and arguments and the actions that follow from them cannot be understood simply in terms of the beliefs and desires of the actors in question. Hacking argues that we must also bring in the style of reasoning in terms of which those claims may be advanced and defended.

This argument poses problems for the principle of charity at two levels. One concerns differences between cultures. If there are distinct styles of reasoning then it may be a mistake to assume, with Davidson, that 'a speaker we do not yet understand is consistent and correct in his beliefs – according to our standards, of course' (Davidson, 1980, p. 238). Different cultures may well have different standards. We understand them by learning how they think, not by assuming that they think as we do. Hacking presents his argument in terms of styles of reasoning because he is concerned with the issue of conceptual relativism, with special reference to the Western scientific tradition. In other words, he is concerned with claims to knowledge and some of the different ways in which they may be proposed and defended. The differences at stake here are differences between cultures or radically different ways of thinking that coexist within a culture. It is in this sense that Hacking writes of where 'we as people have branched off from others as a people' (1982, p. 61) and of 'whole other categories of truth-or-falsehood than ours' (ibid., p. 64).

Differences between cultures or styles of reasoning are certainly important but there is a second issue to be noted here. To say that there are sentences that cannot be understood without reference to some process of deliberation is to say also that there are actions that cannot be understood in terms of the beliefs and desires of the actor alone, without reference also to some process of deliberation. Proposing and defending claims to knowledge are certainly actions, but there are many other actions that depend on some process of deliberation. Deliberation frequently involves the use of specialized techniques or ways of thinking about the issue in question. We shall see that this point is sufficient to undermine the assumption of an holistic rationality.

We may begin with some examples of actions that depend on particular ways of thinking. Here is what Marx and Engels describe as one of the lessons of the Paris Commune: 'the working class cannot simply lay hold of the ready-made state machinery and wield it for its own purposes' (Marx and Engels, 1970, p. 285). Disputes over the interpretation of that statement have played an important part in Marxist debates about the possibility of a democratic road to socialism in the societies of the modern West. These debates need not concern us here.[5] What doe⁵ concern us is that conclusions on this matter have had considerable implications for the actions of revolutionary and social democratic parties.

Marx and Engels's 'lesson' and the debates around its practical implications make sense only in terms of a style of political analysis in which classes are regarded as collective actors with politics as a conflict between them. There are other influential styles of political analysis in which classes are not regarded as political actors: Fabian socialism and the neo-liberalism of sections of the New Right are very different examples. The relations between state and market occupy a central position in each of these styles of political analysis, although they approach those relations in very different ways. At this level they share a distinctly modern view of the national economy both as an object of analysis and as something that can be affected by state action.

There are also forms of political analysis that operate with a different kind of scope, concerning themselves with international relations, the maintenance of political order, crime and regimes of punishment, state responsibilities for the health and welfare of the population, and so on. These diverse styles of political analysis each have some distinctive forms of argument, they start from different premises and they identify issues as important in a variety of different ways. They differ over the questions of what states can or should be expected to do, the interests that states represent, the forces that act upon them, and what can be done to affect their actions. They address different political actors, offer different candidates for possible courses of action and debate them in terms of different considerations.

Now, it would be an exaggeration to treat these different forms of political analysis as involving distinct styles of reasoning in Hacking's sense. Styles of reasoning differ in their candidates for truth and falsehood and how they may be debated. The styles of political analysis considered here would have little difficulty in recognizing many of each other's candidates for truth or falsehood, although they might well reach different conclusions about them. Nevertheless, they are like Hacking's styles of reasoning in the sense that they define fields of debate. They may be characterized by distinctive premisses or beliefs (for example, the belief that classes are, or are not, collective actors) but they cannot be reduced to those beliefs. The class analysis of Marxist socialism provides means of proposing and arguing about possible courses of action. It does not determine what course of action will be chosen in a given situation – as the record of bitter disputes within Marxism makes abundantly clear. Where Hacking's styles of reasoning differ in their candidates for truth or falsehood and how they may be debated, these styles of political analysis differ in the courses of action that may be proposed and the considerations that may be invoked in choosing between them. They do not determine action in the manner of belief in the portfolio model.

Now consider the actions of capitalist enterprises. It is often argued, by Marxist and neo-classical economists alike, that competition results in a process of natural selection operating amongst firms so that the survivors are profit maximizers. Thus, even if managements were not consciously concerned to maximize profit, but aimed instead to satisfice or to be socially responsible or philanthropic towards their workforce, natural selection would nevertheless ensure that in the long run they had no alternative but to act in the manner of profit maximizers.[6] Here 'rationality' is imposed on enterprises by the logic of their situations. In fact it is not difficult to show that there may be conditions in which maximizers and non-maximizers can coexist and others in which maximizers may become extinct (Winter, 1964, 1971, Nelson and Winter, 1982).

More seriously, discussions of profit-maximization tend to proceed as if there were a single correct and unambiguous notion of profit – precisely the one that successful enterprises are supposed to act as if they were pursuing. The problem here is that the notion of profit has no meaning outside of the particular accounting practices in which it is calculated. It will be calculated in different ways for different purposes: taxation, assessment of credit-worthiness, direction of investment within a company, financial scrutiny with a view to asset-stripping, and so on. As for the forms of calculation employed by

companies for their own guidance, these are to a large extent
moulded by national 'rules of the game' set (in Britain) by the
accountancy profession and by the institutional structure of
the national economy (Williams, Williams and Thomas, 1983,
Thompson, 1986).

Even so several distinct modes of calculation may be employed, even by firms operating within a single national economy,
each leading to a different calculation of profit (Cutler *et al.*,
1978, Thompson, 1986). Some of the differences here will be a
matter of the pursuit of different objectives, and others a matter
of different assumptions (for example, about the valuation of
a company's assets). Thus, the assumption that firms set out
to maximize profit does not in itself tell us much about the
practical consequences of that pursuit. We must also consider
the forms of calculation employed by those firms in assessing the
options that appear to be open to them. Sometimes the forms of
calculation employed can have disastrous social consequences
– as the history of British Steel and the National Coal Board
in the 1970s and 1980s shows all too clearly (Williams and
Haslam, 1986).

In these examples decision and action depend in part on
a process of deliberation employing some specialized forms
of analysis and techniques of calculation. Particular areas of
social life (politics, economic activity, the criminal population,
or whatever) are represented as fields of instrumental action.
Both the identification of possible courses of action and the
choice of which one to take involve forms of analysis which are
specialized in the sense that they represent some limited part
of the world as a field of potential action and effects so as to
allow a 'rational' calculation of objectives and how to achieve
them. These forms of analysis certainly depend on assumptions
(beliefs) and on objectives (desires) but they do not relate to
action in the way that belief and desire relate to action in the
portfolio model.

Now the forms of analysis considered here relate to the
conduct of social actors, to states, political parties and capitalist
enterprises. But it is easy enough to find cases in which the
conduct of human individuals depends on deliberation involving
specialized forms of analysis. In Britain at the time of writing

this chapter a number of universities and polytechnics are attempting to train department heads and other senior academics to provide their colleagues with 'academic leadership'. The details of this training need hardly concern us here. It merely adapts forms of training in 'leadership' skills developed elsewhere – in military organizations and management schools. The point to notice is that trainees are provided with specialized techniques of analysis in which the work of their department appears as a field of instrumental action and in which their own behaviour is represented as a means of acting on the behaviour of others. 'Leadership', in this sense, is a specialized skill that can be taught, and its exercise involves deliberation – at least in the early stages. 'Leadership behaviour' does not result simply from the beliefs and desires of the would-be leader.

Two final points should be made before we leave these examples. One is that I have illustrated the role of deliberation by reference to specialized forms of analysis which operate both at the level of the identification of possible courses of action and at the level of the choice between them. But there are also forms of deliberation that take the possible courses of action as given and operate solely at the level of the choice between them. One example would be the use of some more or less sophisticated techniques of cost-benefit analysis in deciding where to locate a new airport or motorway, or whether to allow a proposed nuclear power station to be built. Another would be the use of an oracle or a manual such as the I Ching. In these last, decisions are reached using specialized techniques to produce an answer, and other techniques to interpret how that answer is to be understood.

Finally, although I have emphasized the role of specialized techniques in relation to deliberation, it would be misleading to suggest that specialized techniques have no other place in the determination of action. Mauss argued that 'man's first and most natural technical object, and at the same time technical means, is his body' (Mauss, 1979, p. 104). Human societies differ in their techniques of walking, sleeping (consider the significance of shoes, or of beds and pillows) and other bodily activities. One example of the specificity of techniques is taken from Mauss's experiences in the First World War.

The English troops I was with did not know how to use
French spades, which forced us to change 8,000 spades a
division when we relieved a French division, and vice versa.
This plainly shows that a manual knack can be learnt only
slowly. Every technique properly so called has its own form.
But the same is true of every attitude of the body. Each
society has its own special habits. (ibid., p. 99)

Body techniques are learnt, through imitation in some cases
and as a result of deliberate training in others. Once acquired
they may be taken for granted, but they are not natural. 'This
above all is what distinguishes man from the animals: the
transmission of his techniques' (ibid., p. 104). Body techniques
may not always enter actors' deliberations but they nevertheless
structure the set of possible actions to be considered.

DELIBERATION AND THE ASSUMPTION OF RATIONALITY

At first sight these examples suggest merely that the portfolio
model is incomplete: that the account of action as resulting from
belief and desire must sometimes be supplemented by reference
to the specialized forms of calculation and other techniques
employed by the actor. In fact, their implications go considerably further. Once it is recognized that actors' deliberations
and their use of specialized techniques can play an important
part in the determination of action, then there is no reason to
assume that actors are characterized by an holistic rationality.

I have suggested that the portfolio model of intentional
behaviour suggests a directness in the connection between
actors' beliefs and desires and their behaviour that leaves
little room for those specialized forms of analysis that are
sometimes involved in actors' deliberations. The problem here
is not so much that the place of deliberation in actors' choices
is ignored as that it is treated as unproblematic, as if it were
transparently rational. Action follows from belief and desire
in much the way that the conclusion of an argument follows
from its premisses. On that model actors' deliberations can be
treated as transparent intermediaries between actors' beliefs and
desires on the one hand and their actions on the other.

I have argued, on the contrary, that actors may employ specialized techniques in their deliberations. Simon's discussion of bounded rationality and Hacking's discussion of styles of reasoning suggest two ways in which the 'rationality' of actors' deliberations may differ. Simon's actors satisfice because they have limited cognitive capacities, and we should not be surprised if they satisfice in rather different ways. Hacking's styles of reasoning differ in the candidates for truth-or-falsehood they acknowledge and in how propositions may be advanced and defended. In that sense there are different rationalities. I have taken up and generalized a different implication of Hacking's argument, namely that actors may employ specialized techniques in their deliberations.

To say that actors may employ specialized techniques in their deliberations is to say that action does not always result directly from belief and desire. Instead it results from belief, desire and whatever specialized techniques actors employ in their deliberations. These specialized techniques must then be regarded as possible objects of investigation. This threatens to undermine the portfolio model in several respects. First, the portfolio model implies that the presumption of rationality is necessary if we are to unravel the beliefs and desires of the actor. Once we have identified those beliefs and desires then we are in a position to identify instances of behaviour that are not rational. This dichotomy between rational and irrational behaviour follows from the assumption that what normally intervenes between belief, desire and action is simply the actor's rationality: action will be non-rational when the actor's rationality is not employed correctly.

In fact, what is at issue here is not so much the rationality or otherwise of some particular action, but rather the actor's employment of some definite means of reaching a decision. Once deliberation is involved then questions may be raised both with regard to the identification of the means employed and with regard to how the actor employs them in any given case. Actors may employ what the observer regards as rational means of assessing their situation and deciding on a course of action, and they may employ those means correctly or incorrectly. On the other hand they may employ what the same observer

regards as irrational or inappropriate techniques – say, the I
Ching, cost-benefit analysis, or the poison oracle described in
Evans-Pritchard's account of the Azande. They may employ
those techniques correctly or incorrectly. What matters for
intentional analysis is the techniques employed by actors, not
whether they are rational or otherwise. Once the techniques
employed by some actor or actors in their deliberations have
been identified then, of course, it is possible to identify cases
in which they have not been employed correctly. Intentional
analysis of behaviour requires the identification of any specialized techniques employed in actors' deliberations. It requires
no judgement as to their rationality or otherwise.

Secondly, the possibility of deliberation involving the use
of specialized techniques undermines the requirement that we
assume an holistic rationality. We have seen that Davidson's
principle of charity requires us to suppose that there is a large
measure of consistency and rationality in an actor's behaviour
'according to our own standards, of course' (Davidson, 1980,
p. 238). His argument is that the assumption that action results
from belief and desire commits us to a hermeneutic process
of understanding the behaviour of others. The construction
of our picture of actors' beliefs and desires from observation
of their behaviour in various contexts requires us to presume
a fair degree of rationality and consistency across the board.
The assumption that action results from belief and desire
in turn requires us to make the further assumption of an
holistic rationality. It stands to reason that we could not hope
to interpret actors' beliefs and desires from their behaviour
without the principle of charity or something very like it.

To say that specialized techniques may be involved in actors'
decisions is also to say that the relations between action, belief
and desire may not be the same general character across
the range of their behaviour. In the examples given above
the specialized ways of thinking and techniques of decision-
making relate to particular, limited areas of social life and not
to others. The political analysis of Marxist socialism recognizes
part of the world as a sphere of possible action and effects,
and on that basis is able to identify possible courses of action
and ways of debating the choice between them. The techniques

of 'academic leadership' are concerned with a very different sphere of possible action and effects. The I Ching and oracles may not be specialized in quite the same way (since they are not restricted in their sphere of possible application to any delimited area of social life) but, if they are used at all, they are used only for a limited range of important decisions.

I have already suggested that the problem for the analysis of action is to identify the specialized techniques employed in actors' deliberations – not to pass judgement on their rationality. The point to notice here is a rather different one. Since many of the specialized ways of thinking employed by an actor relate to limited areas of social life, there is no reason to suppose that they will be consistent with each other or that the actor will be particularly concerned if they are not. The academic social scientist may have learned to apply the forms of non-sexist behaviour at work, behave very differently at home – and yet not be aware of any inconsistency. Actors may think differently about different spheres of activity, and there is no need to assume an overall rationality and consistency.

ACTION, BELIEF AND DESIRE

Finally, to question the transparency of relations between action, belief and desire is also to undermine the idea that actors must be characterized in terms of a more or less stable portfolio of beliefs and desires. I argued in chapter 4 that beliefs and desires should be attributed to actors as part of some intentional process only if they can be formulated by the actor in question. Interests, beliefs and desires that cannot be formulated by an actor play no part in the intentional explanation of that actor's behaviour. The beliefs and desires that do play a part in an actor's behaviour will depend on the availability to that actor of the conceptual means of formulating them. My point here is not that the formulation of particular beliefs and desires depends on possession of a conceptual scheme in the sense that Davidson quite rightly attacks. The point rather is that there are specialized ways of thinking, some of which represent part of the world as a sphere of action and effects. Some beliefs and some desires will depend on the use of such specialized ways of thinking. At any given time, many of these will be available to some actors and not to others. This means that at least some of the beliefs and desires of actors will themselves depend on specialized techniques and ways of thinking that are clearly not inherent features of the actors themselves.

The character of interests, beliefs and desires as formulations renders them open to challenge through reconsideration by the actor concerned and through discussion, propaganda and persuasion involving others. Such challenges will not always be effective, of course, but the fact that they are successful in some cases means that actors' beliefs and desires cannot be regarded as given elements of their consciousnesses until something drastic comes along to change them.

Now, these points go along with the portfolio model in taking the actor's beliefs and desires as the appropriate starting-point for the explanation of behaviour. They challenge it by suggesting that the portfolio should be expanded to include specialized techniques and ways of thinking, and that at least some elements of an actor's portfolio may be more open to change than the model suggests. But the model should also be questioned from another direction. Intentional analysis supposes that actors employ some means of assessing situations and deciding on courses of action. I have presented the issue as if the actor possesses certain beliefs and desires which are brought into some definite process of deliberation, possibly involving specialized techniques, leading to a decision about behaviour.

The difficulty here is that there are cases where the attribution of belief to the actor can be misleading. There is a good example of this in Evans-Pritchard's account of his own behaviour during his fieldwork amongst the Azande. He was firmly convinced of the falsity of Zande beliefs regarding witchcraft and the poison oracle. Nevertheless, he reports himself as sometimes reacting to misfortune in the idiom of witchcraft – behaviour that he regarded as a 'lapse into unreason' (Evans-Pritchard, 1976, p. 45). He also reports that he kept a supply of poison for the use of his household and neighbours, and that

> we regulated our affairs in accordance with the oracle's decisions. I may remark that I found this as satisfactory a

way of running my home and affairs as any other I know
of. (ibid., p. 126)

But it would be misleading to present that behaviour as resulting
from his belief in witchcraft.

This example illustrates a more general issue. Specialised
ways of thinking and techniques employed in actors' deliberations may well require certain 'beliefs' as premises – for
example, the beliefs involved in reading the poison oracle.
But it need not follow that those beliefs are held by actors
who employ those modes of assessment and act upon them.
Evans-Pritchard describes himself as sometimes acting on the
basis of beliefs that he did not hold. From a rather different
perspective Weber's account of the effects of rationalization
suggests that action of this kind is a pervasive feature of the
modern world.[7]

There are other cases where actors may not even be aware
of the premises of the ways of thinking and techniques that
they employ. In chapter 2 I quoted the following passage from
Keynes's *General Theory*:

the ideas of economists and political philosophers ... are
more powerful than is commonly understood. Indeed the
world is ruled by little else. Practical men who believe themselves to be quite exempt from any intellectual influences,
are usually slaves of some defunct economist. (Keynes,
1936, p. 383)

Keynes's remark is unduly restrictive. Similar points could be
made about defunct mathematicians, scientists, social reformers
and many others. Think of our use of the achievements of
Greek geometry and the mathematization of the physical world
that we have inherited from the seventeenth century,[8] or of
the parameters of modern debates on crime and punishment
(Foucault, 1977).

Action will often involve premises which could not reasonably be described as propositional attitudes held by the actor
concerned. Putting the point rather loosely, we could say that
in such cases action depends on beliefs and desires that are

not those of the actor. The point here is not to deny that the actor's beliefs and desires are ever an appropriate starting point for intentional analysis. The patterning of behaviour that starts from actors' beliefs and desires and moves out from them obviously plays an important part in social life – or at least in our perception of it. The point rather is that much of intentional behaviour, involving calculation and deliberation, has a more complex form.

6
Individualism and social structure

Where do the arguments of this book leave us? Rational choice analysis insists that actors do indeed make choices and act on them, and that much of what happens in society can be understood as the outcome of strategic interactions between intentional actors – that is, it does not result from the workings of some overarching social structure. One of the appeals of this approach lies in its claim to theoretical parsimony: the ability to produce powerful results (in public choice theory, the analysis of government taxation and spending policies, the construction of a game-theoretical Marxism) on the basis of relatively simple theoretical foundations. As a mode of social explanation rational choice analysis involves an explicit methodological individualism and a distinctive model of the individual actor. I have argued that it is seriously deficient in both respects and further that many of its apparently powerful results depend on an implicit structural determinism with regard to actors' forms of thought. This concluding chapter surveys the implications of these arguments and the final section returns to the issues of parsimony and the purposes of social analysis.

METHODOLOGICAL INDIVIDUALISM

I noted in chapter 2 that Elster presents 'the principle of methodological individualism, not infrequently violated by Marx' as nevertheless 'underlying much of his most important work' (Elster, 1985, p. 4). The converse to that principle is structuralism or methodological collectivism, based on the assumption that 'there are supra-individual entities that are prior to the

individual in the explanatory order. Explanation proceeds from
the laws either of self-regulation or of development of these
larger entities, while individual actions are derived from the
aggregate pattern' (ibid., p. 6). As Elster describes it methodological collectivism assumes that such larger entities operate by
closing off the options available to the actor, so that nothing is
left to choice.

Elsewhere (Elster, ed., 1986, p. 23) he suggests a further
possible alternative to methodological individualism, namely
that action might be understood in terms of the acting out
of *social* norms rather than of *individual* rationality. However,
in Elster's account this turns out to be another, albeit less
powerful, means of subordinating individuals to determination
by a supra-individual entity. Where collectivism leaves actors
no choice, the operation of norms interferes with their decision-
making but does not entirely determine it. (Norms, like laws,,
are made to be broken.) Elster does not entirely reject the
idea that actors may be subject to norms, but he does insist
that explanation in terms of norms should be considered only
after attempts at rational explanation have clearly failed. In so
far as they are rational, then, actors are not subordinated to
supra-individual forces.

At first sight, the fundamental objection of rational choice
analysis to what Elster describes as structuralism and methodological collectivism follows directly from its view of the
paradigmatic status of the assumption of rationality. If we
are to consider other explanations only after explanation in
rational terms has clearly failed, then we can hardly assume that
action is subordinated to the requirements of some overarching
social totality.

However, there is a more general objection to be noted
here which is in no way peculiar to rational choice analysis.
Indeed, the idea that actors' behaviour can be derived from
their positions in some larger pattern is incompatible with all
of the models of actor considered in the last two chapters. The
concept of actor as making decisions and acting on them cannot
be reconciled with a concept of society as a functioning whole
governed by some unifying principle (for example, by a central
value system or dominant mode of production) and producing

necessary effects by virtue of its structural exigencies. If actors do indeed act on their decisions there can be no reason to expect their actions to accord with the requirements of society as a functioning whole.

The strictures of rational choice analysis on this point seem to me entirely justified, but it is thoroughly misleading to present the issue as if we had to choose between methodological individualism on the one hand and what Elster describes as collectivism on the other. First, I noted in chapter 3 that discussions of methodological individualism frequently confuse two quite distinct debates. One concerns the subordination of individuals to the functioning of supra-individual processes and the other concerns the dependence of actors on social conditions of various kinds. It is entirely possible to argue that individuals are irreducible to the effects of social structure and to insist that social life is not reducible to their actions. Methodological individualism and collectivism have never been the only forms of social analysis on offer, and the opposition between structure and agency has always been widely disputed.[1]

Secondly, for all their apparent opposition there is also a certain complicity between these positions. I have already suggested that there is an implicit structuralism in the apparently powerful reductions of structural phenomena to effects of actors' rationality that we find, say, in Olson's discussions of collective action or Elster's reconstruction of Marxism. I return to this issue below. For the moment, consider what methodological individualism and collectivism have in common. On the one side we are presented with the human individual as creative subject, freely constituting its actions and thereby constituting and reconstituting social relations in the process. On the other there is the human individual as literally the subject of its place in the system of social relations: it internalizes its part and subsequently acts it out. What is shared here is a conception of the human subject as characterized by attributes of will and subjectivity, conceived as a condition of its creative activity in the one case and as the means of its subjection to its position in the structure in the other.[2] Both are reductionist in the sense that they propose to reduce social conditions of diverse kinds to others that are alleged to be more basic, either to specific structural conditions (dominant values, the needs of capital, or whatever) or to the creative activity of individuals.

Returning now to the main argument, I have suggested that actors reach decisions and act on many of them, so that their actions result in part from their decisions. The decisions themselves are reached through deliberation and through other processes that are internal to the actor in question. In that respect they are clearly irreducible to the effects of the actor's position in some larger structure or system of social relations. So far, so good. The trouble with the rational choice critique of structuralism and methodological collectivism is that what it offers as the alternative turns on a very limited notion of the implications for action of social relations and of conditions that are external to the individual actor.

In contrast to the methodological individualism of rational choice analysis I have argued first that there are actors other than human individuals, and secondly that actors' decisions and actions depend on conditions that are external to the actor concerned. I return to social actors below. As for the second point, I have concentrated in this book on the role of the specialized techniques and ways of thinking that may be employed by actors in evaluating the conditions they confront and deciding on a course of action – precisely because their significance is obscured by theories that assume an inherent rationality on the part of the actor. But similar points could be made by reference to conditions of other kinds.

It is trivially true, for example, that the action of social actors depends on the actions of others. Human individuals may not be the constitutive subjects of social life, but they are the only actors whose actions do not invariably depend on the actions of others. Nevertheless, many of the most significant kinds of action clearly depend on conditions that are external to the acting individual. The actions of capitalist employers depend on certain legal rights over the disposition of property and over what employees may be required to do or not to do. They may also depend on the use of various control techniques involving hierarchical chains of command and supervision, the collection and processing of information and so on. In this example, the means of action that crucially distinguish the position of the capitalist (whether human individual or corporation) from that of an employee depend precisely on their differential location within several intersecting sets of social relations.

To say that actors' decisions are not reducible to effects of their positions in some larger structure or system is to say simply that there are no essential structures of social life provided by the operations of society as a self-sustaining totality. It is not to say that the patterns of social interaction are essentially fragile and unpredictable, or that actors have *carte blanche* to change the world as they will. Actors make decisions and act accordingly, but they do so under conditions that are only partly under their control, and on the basis of the techniques, ways of thinking, and means of action available to them. What those conditions, means of action and ways of thinking are is a matter of choice only to a limited extent. Actors may work to change how they (and others) think, but they cannot adopt entirely new ways of thinking quickly or at will.

CONCEPTS OF ACTOR

Actors use tools for thinking, and what results depends on the tools, on how they are used and on what they are used to work on. The tools may be simple or complex, their use may be commonplace in a particular society or community or they may be relatively specialized. Similarly for the materials that are worked on. Some tools will make use of others or presuppose their existence. Most of the specialized tools used in academic work, for example, make use of the relatively commonplace skills of reading and writing. Within a society individuals and groups may differ in the specialized tools they are able to use or are in a position to acquire. Societies themselves may differ in the tools that are widely used within them and in the tools that are more specialized.

Where literacy is widespread there will also be specialized techniques of storing, retrieving and working with written materials, and various distinctive uses of written materials in relation to other activities (the experimental sciences, business management, government bureaucracies and so on). Specialized styles of literary work may develop in which the products of earlier work provide both tools and materials to work on. Non-literate societies will have their own techniques for storing, retrieving and working with ideas and information. Some of these will be widely used, while others may be specialized and restricted. In any society there will be many tools whose use is normally taken for granted and which provide the basis for a variety of others that may (or may not) be acquired later on. Most will be acquired relatively early in life, either along the way in the course of interaction with others or through more deliberate training. Many specialized tools build on or elaborate the use of others, which have to be acquired first. Most intellectual skills, and much of what counts as intelligence, involve interrelated skills of this kind. Those who miss out on some of the more commonplace tools may be severely disadvantaged when it comes to the use or acquisition of others.[3]

In effect, I have argued that the tools used by actors in their thinking, their interrelationships and their dependence on social conditions of various kinds are legitimate and important areas of investigation. Human societies have developed an enormous variety of such tools (the poison oracle, the straws and manual of I Ching, several kinds of writing, number systems and geometries, cost-benefit analysis, Aristotelian physics, neo-classical and Marxist economics, song, ritual and mythology, rational choice analysis, and many others) and of purposes for which they may be used. The kinds of questions actors pose for themselves and the conclusions they are able to reach will depend on the tools they are in a position to employ. In the latter part of this book I have used the terms 'techniques' and 'forms of thought' loosely to refer quite generally to the tools that actors employ in the course of their deliberations.

The portfolio model admits little of the variety and complexity sketched here, and rational choice analysis admits even less. I have argued against the latter by questioning its refinements of the portfolio model and by disputing the portfolio model itself. The refinement most frequently noted involves the adoption of a restricted utilitarian conception of actors' rationality. We saw in chapter 3 that critics have advanced powerful arguments for a more complex view of actors' rationality. But perhaps the most important refinement concerns not the adoption of some particular conception of rationality, but rather the claim that the assumption of rationality should have a paradigmatic status in the explanation of action. It is one thing to insist, with the portfolio model, that we can only make sense of the beliefs and desires of actors if we assume that they are by and large rational. It is quite another, I have argued, to insist on a general presumption of rationality in the case of any behaviour that we might wish to explain. The claim to paradigmatic status raises important questions, concerning the purposes of social analysis and its political implications, to which I return in the final section of this conclusion.

As for the portfolio model itself, I have proposed a still more general model of the actor and have argued, in particular, against its presumption that actors are characterized by an holistic rationality. An actor is a locus of decision and action, and in that sense there are important actors in the world other than human individuals. In many cases decision and action involve the application of specialized techniques whose role in actors' deliberations and actions is obscured by the presumption of an holistic rationality. I have developed these arguments primarily with reference to rational choice analysis, but versions of the portfolio model are widely used in social theory and the consequences of challenging it have more general implications. There is no space here to deal with these implications at length, but it may be worth commenting briefly on two other models of the actor and on the concept of social actor.

First, I noted in chapter 4 that Weber's model of the actor is that of a human individual motivated by a mixture of material interests and ideal interests (values). There is no suggestion here that the overall pattern of desires has a utilitarian structure. Quite the contrary: not only will the demands of material and ideal interests sometimes pull in contrary directions but different ideal interests will come into conflict with each other. Weber's version of the portfolio model is therefore rather different from that of rational choice analysis. Nevertheless, Weber too insists that the assumption of rationality should have a paradigmatic status. His claim is not that action is always rational, far from it, but rather that the place of non-rational elements in behaviour can be seen as accounting for deviations from rational action. In this respect, the model of the actor presented in Weber's methodological writings, like those of rational choice analyses, forecloses serious questions of the forms of deliberation employed by actors and the conditions on which they depend, and it imposes a restrictive and unnecessary psychic unity on to the conception of actor.

Secondly, consider Giddens's account of agents in *The Constitution of Society*. The introduction complains that a 'good deal of social theory, especially that associated with structural sociology, has treated agents as much less knowledgeable than they really are'(Giddens, 1984, p. xxx). The sense in which he supposes agents to be knowledgeable is made clear in a later discussion. He admits that actors can be wrong:

> But if there is to be any continuity to social life at all, most actors must be right most of the time; that is to say they know what they are doing, and they successfully communicate their knowledge to others. The knowledgeability incorporated in the practical activities which make up the bulk of daily life is a constitutive feature (together with power) of the social world. (ibid., p. 90)

It is a common rhetorical manoeuvre to maintain that the only alternative to the author's suggestion is chaos. Parsons' use of 'the problem of order' to shore up his treatment of systems of action is perhaps the best-known example in the history of sociology: if social systems were not homeostatic and boundary-maintaining entities, how could there be order in social life? Here Giddens uses the problem of 'continuity' to similar effect: if actors were not right most of the time and did not successfully communicate with others, how could there be any continuity to social life at all? We should not be misled by the 'obviousness' of his answer.

Ethnomethodology and phenomenological sociology have stressed knowledgeability in order to counter the idea that actors are 'cultural dopes', merely following the dictates of their position in the structure of society, and Giddens continues in that tradition. Now, I have argued that actors do indeed make decisions and act on them, and that their decisions should not be seen as reflecting their position in some overarching social structure. Actors deliberate about their situation using particular techniques and ways of thinking and they make decisions on the basis of a practical consciousness. So far, then, we are in agreement. But why should we assume that 'most actors must be right most of the time', let alone that they successfully communicate their knowledge to others?

Giddens's thesis of actors' knowledgeability is not unlike Davidson's principle of charity – the claim that we should regard actors as generally consistent and correct in their beliefs – although they would argue these positions in rather different ways. In both cases the effect is to render actors' deliberations of little interest. Where the thesis of holistic rationality requires us to treat actors' deliberations as transparently rational most of the time the thesis of knowledgeability would have us treat them as transparently correct. In both cases actors' deliberations become the focus of interest only in those situations where the thesis appears to break down.

The problem is not that Giddens has nothing to say about actors' forms of thought, but rather that what he does have to say is severely constrained by the prior assumption of knowledgeability. If actors are right most of the time, then what has to be investigated is not so much the techniques and ways of thinking employed by some particular actor or actors, but rather the limits to their knowledgeability. Giddens therefore goes on to consider 'the types of circumstance that tend to influence the level and nature of the "penetration" actors have of the conditions of system reproduction'(ibid., p. 91). It is here that Giddens locates the primary connection between actors' forms of thought and power: actors' knowledge is limited by the operations of power. Of course it is! The weakness of Giddens's argument at this point is that it involves a restricted view both of power and of the ways in which actors' knowledge may relate to social conditions.[4]

In fact, just as the explanation of behaviour requires no judgement as to the rationality of the techniques and ways of thinking employed in actors' deliberations, so it requires no assumption that their 'knowledge' is most of the time correct. In order to analyse what actors do we must consider the techniques, ways of thinking and practical knowledge they employ in reaching their decisions and deciding on courses of action. Actors act on the decisions they take, whatever those decisions happen to be, and they take those decisions on the basis of what they 'know', not on the basis of whether what they 'know' is true. If we are concerned with accounting for their actions then the question of the rationality of those decisions and the truth of the 'knowledge' involved are of no explanatory significance. In cases where actors were irrational or mistaken it might well be that they would have acted differently had they known better – but that is merely to say that they might have acted otherwise had they thought differently about their situation.

Of course, actors require some means of making sense of situations that confront them and of deciding on objectives and courses of action. But there is no reason to suppose that the 'knowledge' involved here is generally correct. What matters rather is that it provides some way of coming to terms with the all too common failure of things to turn out as expected. There are academics and political activists in most Western societies who analyse politics at least in part in terms of a struggle between classes. There are others who analyse things in terms of some version of rational choice. The continued survival of these forms of analysis depends not so much on their truth as on their ability to provide adherents with some way of coming to terms with the all too common experiences of practical or explanatory failure, and with the aftermath of their occasional success (Hindess, 1987a, 1988). I will return to this point.

SOCIAL ACTORS

Chapter 4 presented a minimal concept of actor as locus of decision and action. Human individuals are certainly actors in that sense, but they are not alone. Now, the idea that there are important actors in the modern world other than human individuals is widely accepted, but it is likely to be understood in several different ways. Two influential interpretations in particular should be avoided. The first is the treatment of social actors as if they were themselves reducible to human individuals. Weber's explicit methodological individualism is the most obvious example, but there are many others.[5]

There are usually two aspects to the claim that social actors are reducible to human individuals, as if the latter were the only real actors. One concerns the attribution of a unitary subjectivity to humans, but not to other actors. I noted in chapter 4, for example, that the decisions of corporate actors are frequently dispersed within the organization.[6] We are concerned, say, with the pattern of investment displayed by a large corporation, and we try to understand that behaviour as resulting from a mixture of standing policies and recent decisions. Intentional analysis in this case is hardly going to lead us in the direction of interpreting those policies as resulting from the consistent application of some more or less stable collection of beliefs and desires. Decisions are made and policies laid down at a variety of points within the organization, and we are more likely to interpret them in terms of the application of particular accounting practices, institutionalized techniques of information-gathering and assessment, decision-making procedures, and their relationships to decisions and policies emanating from elsewhere.

The decisions of corporations and other social actors should not be seen as the products of a unitary consciousness. Yes – but we should be wary of the presumption that the decisions of human individuals are not themselves the dispersed products of diverse and sometimes conflicting objectives, forms of calculation and means of action. One advantage of the minimal concept of actor proposed in chapter 4 is that it forces us to consider the processes by which decisions are produced, by humans as much as by social actors, rather than simply refer them to a supposed unitary subjectivity.

The other aspect concerns the point that the actions of social actors always depend on those of others – executives, managerial and other employees, elected officials, legal representatives, and sometimes other social actors. I have called them 'social actors' precisely because each and every one of their actions involves social relations with other actors. Does it follow that they can be discounted as actors on the grounds that their actions always involve the actions of human individuals? We have seen that decision and action depend on conditions that are external to the actor in question, so that social relations cannot be reduced to the constitutive activity of those engaged in them. Social actors always depend on social relationships involving others but they are not constituted by those others, and there is no reason to suppose that human individuals will be the only others involved.

But the most important point to notice here is that even if there were a sense in which the actions of social actors could always be reduced to those of human individuals, we should still be concerned with investigating their conditions of action and with the consequences of their decisions and actions. Considered in terms of their social impact, many of the most significant decisions in the modern world are taken by social actors – by governments, large corporations, unions, churches. If we were to treat human individuals as the only real actors then these social actors would have to be regarded not so much as actors, but rather as the instruments of some other set of interests. Much of the debate over the alleged separation of corporate ownership from its control is beset by that confusion.[7] To say that human individuals are not the only real actors is to argue, on the contrary, that social actors should be regarded as actors with concerns and objectives of their own. It may be possible to subject these actors to controls and restrictions of various kinds, and some of them could no doubt be dispensed with without any great loss to the rest of us. But it is impossible to conceive of a complex modern society in which social actors did not play a major role. Any approach to the analysis of modern societies that admits only human individuals as effective actors must be regarded as seriously incomplete.

The second influential but misleading view concerns those extensions of the concept of actor to cover things that are actors in only the most allegorical of senses: classes, societies, men as a collectivity subordinating women as another collectivity, and so on. These are all spurious actors, and they are frequently invoked in political and social scientific discourses. In particular, the analysis of politics in terms of relations between competing classes usually involves one or both of two elements. One is a notion of classes as collective actors. The other is a conception of class interests as objectively given to individuals by virtue of their social location, and therefore as providing a basis for action in common.

There are many well-known problems with the idea of structurally determined class interests, but it is the idea of classes as collective *actors* that particularly concerns us here. The trouble with this notion, as I argued in chapter 4, is that even a minimal concept of actor requires that the actor possess means of taking decisions and of acting on them. Capitalist enterprises, state agencies, trade unions and community associations are all examples of actors in this minimal sense – that is, they all possess means of taking decisions and of acting on at least some of them. There are other collectivities, such as classes and societies, that have no identifiable means of taking decisions, let alone of acting on them. There are, of course, actors who claim to take decisions and to act on behalf of classes and other collectivities, but the very diversity of such claims is reason to be wary about accepting any one of them.

The point of restricting the concept of actor to things that take decisions and act on some of them is simply that actors' decisions are an important part of the explanation of their actions. To apply the concept of actor to classes or other collectivities that have no means of taking decisions and acting on them, and then to explain some state of affairs (say, the emergence of the welfare state or its current crisis[8]) as resulting from their actions is to indulge in a kind of fantasy. Such fantastic explanations may well be thought to serve a polemical function, but they can only obscure our understanding of the state of affairs in question, and political decisions as to what can or should be done about them.

RATIONALITY AND ACTORS' DELIBERATIONS

I suggested earlier that the apparently powerful reductions of structural phenomena to effects of actors' rationality in, say, Olson's discussions of collective action or Elster's reconstruction of Marxism are themselves products of an implicit structuralism.

The explanation of social conditions in terms of the actions of large numbers of individual actors requires some account of how their actions have been co-ordinated so as to produce precisely the aggregate effects to be explained. This is not a problem for what Elster would call methodological collectivism since it claims to rely on the action of the structure to achieve the appropriate result. In effect, it treats interests (or norms and values) as if they derived from actors' social location on the one hand and as if they played a crucial role in determining their decisions and actions on the other. The actions of large numbers of individuals come together to produce structural effects because the structure itself makes sure that they do.

Rational choice analysis will have nothing to do with such structural determination – and quite right too, as we have seen. Instead, it relies on actors' rationality to ensure that their actions are suitably co-ordinated, sometimes invoking the tale of the unintended consequence to explain how the trick is done. We have seen that the latter plays an important part in Elster's reconstruction of Marx's social thought, but it is of little explanatory value. It is a matter of everyday experience that actions have unintended consequences, and the idea that they do so is a commonplace of Western social thought. To say that an economic crisis is the unintended consequence of the actions of millions of individual capitalists and workers is to say merely that those millions did not intend to bring about the crisis that resulted from their actions. The observation is not without merit, but it does not suffice to explain why they behaved as they did.

As for the assumption of rationality at the level of each individual actor, how could that be sufficient to explain specific structural phenomena or social conditions? The problem here is simply that the assumption of rationality in any of the senses discussed in this book tells us little about what actors will do, other than that there will be a certain kind of consistency in their behaviour. The 'explanation' of collective outcomes and social structural phenomena as resulting from the rational actions of large numbers of individual actors must therefore involve some combination of two possible forms. The first is an empty gesture, asserting yet again that the actors are indeed rational and explaining nothing – since whatever outcome had occurred it would still have been the result of their rational actions.

The other is a surreptitious structural determination which assumes a distribution of beliefs and desires throughout society such that an important part of what rational actors do may be regarded as determined by a logic inscribed in the social conditions in which they find themselves. More precisely, what is to count as rational action for some particular actor is a function of that actor's membership of one of the social categories recognized by the rational choice model under consideration: capitalists behave as they do because they are capitalists and because they are rational, similarly for their employees, consumers and everyone else.

We saw in chapter 2, for example, how Elster attributes the counterfinality of capitalist production to the fact that capitalists in general fail to engage in a fully strategic rationality. Instead they act rationally on the basis of irrational assumptions about the behaviour of other capitalists – that is, each decides to act differently on the assumption that the other capitalists will continue as before. Why are they all so foolish? The argument requires that capitalists are constrained to act as they do because of what seems rational to them by virtue of their social location. Marx's structural determination is thrown out of the front door, and quietly brought back in again through the rear.

Elster's undermining of his own methodological individualism is but one instance of a more general phenomenon. Since the assumption of actors' rationality tells us nothing about the substance of their concerns, any explanation of collective outcomes as resulting from their rational actions or the respective 'logics' of their situations clearly requires some further assumption about the social distribution of those concerns. This last, of course, contradicts the explicit assumption of methodological individualism. It is usually smuggled in as part of the definition of the categories of actor recognized by the model. A model of electoral competition, for example, may recognize the distinct categories of leaders, activists, and actual or potential voters. It will then generate results by assigning a particular distribution of preferences and a mode of political calculation to members of each category.

The problem here lies in the assumption that the concerns of rational actors are determined by the social categories to which they belong. Rational political leaders have certain concerns by virtue of their status as leaders, rational capitalists have certain concerns by virtue of their status as capitalists, and so on. The construction of rational choice models of political and economic life presupposes a 'structural' determination of the forms of thought employed by actors, at least in so far as they are rational. Structural accounts of individual action and rational choice analyses use different theoretical means to produce the same overall result: what actors do is determined by their social location, through the action of the structure in the one case and through the effects of actors' rationality in the other.

Now, I have argued that the problem with the assumption of actors' rationality is that it thoroughly obscures questions of the techniques and ways of thinking employed in actors' deliberations. This is a problem for the portfolio model in general, but rational choice analysis adds several complications of its own: first, the implicit structural determinism noted above, secondly the assumption of a utilitarian pattern of desires so that rational actors normally engage in maximizing behaviour, and thirdly the supposed paradigmatic status of the assumption of rationality. Leaving those complications to one side, the problem for the portfolio model here is not so much that the place of deliberation in actors' choices is ignored as that it is regarded as unproblematic, as if it were transparently rational. In effect, action is supposed to follow from belief and desire in much the way that the conclusion of an argument follows from its premisses. On that model actors' deliberations can be treated as transparent intermediaries between actors' beliefs and desires on the one hand and their actions on the other.

The portfolio model of intentional behaviour suggests a directness in the connection between actors' beliefs and desires and their behaviour that leaves little room for those specialized forms of analysis that are sometimes involved in actors' deliberations. To suggest that those specialized techniques should themselves be regarded as possible objects of investigation is to undermine the portfolio model of intentional behaviour in several respects. First, there is the claim that the presumption of rationality is necessary if we are to be able to identify actors' beliefs and desires starting from our observations of their behaviour. We have seen that this claim depends on the assumption that what normally intervenes between belief and desire on the one hand and action on the other is simply the actor's rationality. I argued to the contrary in chapter 5 that the intentional analysis of behaviour requires the identification of the particular techniques employed in actors' deliberations. It requires no judgement as to their rationality.

Secondly, to say that actors' deliberations may involve the use of specialized techniques or ways of thinking is to say that the relations between action, belief and desire need not be of the same general character across the whole range of an actor's behaviour. Chapter 5 considered several examples of specialized ways of thinking which relate to particular, limited areas of social life. There is therefore no reason to suppose that the techniques and ways of thinking employed by an actor will be consistent with each other. This point undermines the portfolio model's assumption of an holistic rationality. Actors may well think differently in different areas of activity, and there is no reason to suppose that they are by and large rational and consistent.

If, contrary to these arguments, we were to assume that actors were rational by virtue of their status as actors, or merely that they should be treated as such in our attempts to analyse their behaviour, then there would be no reason to enquire further into the techniques and forms of thought employed in their deliberations. They think as they do because they are rational and further, in rational choice accounts, because they belong to the category of political leader, capitalist entrepreneur, or whatever. To dispute the assumption of rationality is therefore to raise questions concerning the techniques and forms of thought employed by or available to actors and questions of the social conditions on which they depend.

SOCIAL LOCATION

One set of questions, to which I return briefly below, concerns the survival and social significance of particular forms of thought. Another concerns the conditions affecting their availability to or employment by particular actors. The cultural and educational diversity of most societies ensures that there will be considerable variation in the forms of thought employed by or available to actors. We may begin by disposing of the idea that such differences in the forms of thought employed by actors can be accounted for as reflecting their interests or some aspect of their social location. The latter returns us to the structural determinism I have already rejected. As for interests, I have argued that there is no possibility of interests (or norms and values) operating as mere transmissions between social structure and actors' decisions. Interests have consequences only in so far as they enter actors' deliberations and contribute towards providing them with reasons for action (Hindess, 1986b). Interests in this sense have to be formulated or capable of formulation by those who act on them – which is to say that the existence of interests depends on the forms of thought available to actors. There is therefore a significant element of circularity in any suggestion that actors' forms of thought reflect their interests.

This is not to say, of course, that there are no connections between the techniques and forms of thought available to actors and their social location. In any society there will be reasonably clear cultural differences (i.e. differences in forms of thought employed by actors) which relate to features of its social structure. The point is simply that these patterns should not be seen as reflecting any general mechanism of determination of forms of thought by social structure. There are many different ways in which the forms of thought employed by or available to actors may be related to their social location, and I shall give some examples in a moment, but what the connections are in any given case will have to be a matter for investigation.

To say that there is no general mechanism of determination of actors' forms of thought by their social structural location is to say that the relations between them will depend on features of both. Perhaps the most obvious connection is that the occupation of a social position involves engaging in a range of activities associated with that position. It therefore involves the techniques and forms of thought required to perform those activities. This is particularly clear in the case of professions and other more or less skilled occupations requiring specialized training, but it applies far more generally – in fact to anything that depends on socialization. Here features of the forms of thought employed by actors can certainly be read off from their social position, but it would be thoroughly misleading to talk of determination of the one by the other.

A rather different kind of connection follows from the fact that many techniques and forms of thought are preconditions for the acquisition of others. I argued above that some specialized techniques build on or elaborate other techniques which have to be acquired first. Even where that is not the case, access to training may be restricted to those who can demonstrate their possession of certain skills. Or again, actors' current beliefs, concerns and preoccupations condition what specialized techniques and forms of thought seem worthwhile acquiring or investigating further. For example, all employees in a manufacturing enterprise may be affected by its investment strategy (if there is one), but they would not all be affected in the same way and they are not equally well placed to influence that strategy. Senior managers and wage-labourers are therefore likely to have very different attitudes towards the acquisition of the accountancy and other skills involved in formulating and evaluating long-term financial strategies. To take a different example, barristers and other professionals may find it difficult to locate themselves in terms of a class-based socialist discourse. In these ways the social distribution of some techniques and forms of thought has consequences for the social distribution of others.

Does this argument about the differential availability of specialized techniques and forms of thought mean that the role of transmission mechanism between social structure and individual action has merely been displaced – from interests, beliefs and desires in the one case to techniques and forms of thought in the other? The answer is no for two reasons. First the outcomes of actors' deliberations depend on complex internal processes which may vary considerably from one actor to another. There are differences between human individuals, between human and social actors, and, of course, between social actors themselves. The outcomes of actors' deliberations are not determined solely by the techniques and forms of thought they employ. Secondly, in the complex societies of the modern world (and perhaps in all societies) the techniques and forms of thought employed by actors are not uniquely determined by their social location. What is available to an actor may not be used and some of the limitations on what is available may be changed – for example, through education or specialized training. Nevertheless, what could be employed by an actor at any given time is never entirely a matter of choice, and where there is an element of choice that will be structured by the forms of thought available to that actor. There are always connections of various kinds between actors' social locations and the techniques and forms of thought they employ in deciding on courses of action, but there is no simple correspondence between them.

TALES OF RATIONAL ECONOMIC MAN

What can we say of the conditions affecting the survival and social significance of particular forms of thought? If there is no general mechanism of determination of actors' forms of thought by their social structural location, then there is little to be said in general about the conditions affecting their survival or social impact. There are numerous different ways in which the forms of thought employed by actors may be related to other forms of thought and to features of their social location. Many of them will be clear to anyone familiar with the society in question. It would be necessary to trace those relations for the form of thought in question in order to account for its survival or social impact.

However, there is one form of thought whose survival and social significance should be considered in this concluding chapter. I noted above that there are academics and political activists who analyse politics, at least in part, in terms of some notion of class struggle. There are others who do so in terms of rational individual actors. In the academic social sciences and in much of economic and political life tales of rational economic man and his more or less close relations are far more influential than tales of classes and the struggles between them. Systematic argument certainly plays its part in some of these tales, but it would be a rationalist illusion to imagine that the influence or survival of either of these doctrines depends primarily on their objectivity or coherence. I have discussed the explanatory pretensions of class analysis elsewhere (Hindess, 1987a), but what of the model of rational economic man and related conceptions of the actor? How could such inadequate conceptualizations nevertheless play such an important part in the modern world?

Notice first that the significance of the presumption of rationality is not a matter of 'realism', in the sense of approximating to an accurate description of how people behave. Models of rational economic man and his descendants may have emerged in the developing capitalist societies of the West, but they do not have their origins in careful observation of human behaviour, and they will not disappear merely because they can be shown to be inadequate. In academic life we have seen that few advocates of the rational choice approach would claim that their model of the actor was entirely realistic. On the contrary, it is said to be useful in spite of its lack of realism. I will return to that claim.

In other spheres of social activity it is clear that the test of falsifiability is not a significant element in the life of such doctrines – any more than it is in the case of class analysis. In the case of the presumption of rationality, what is at stake is not just a matter of popular belief in particular economic or political theories, in some more or less elaborate construction based on rational economic man and his [*sic*] close relations. It is also a matter of concepts of the person that play an important part in the social life of modern societies: for example, in the forms of criminal and civil law, in our conceptions of contract and the wage labour relationship, and in many of our assumptions about the organization and content of education (Hirst and Woolley, 1982). Concepts of the person as rational actor are significant components of the social life of modern societies rather than accurate reflections of what goes on within them.

If realism is not necessarily to be expected of these tales of rational economic man and his descendants, they must nevertheless have a certain plausibility. In other words, they must provide those who use them with some purchase on the situations in which they are supposed to apply. They must provide means of assessing those situations, of deciding on objectives to pursue within them, of identifying potential obstacles and deciding what to do about them. What they must also do, of course, is to provide means of coming to terms with the all too common experience of practical and explanatory failure. Any reasonably complex body of contemporary social thought provides resources appropriate to these purposes, and that associated with the presumption of rationality is no exception.

In the case of rational economic man and his descendants, it must be possible to represent the relevant aspects of human behaviour in terms of the actions of such persons, and to have some means of accounting for actions that fail to conform – for example, through concepts of mental disability, illness and incapacity, affectual and other non-rational sources of motivation, and so on. The proposal that we treat models of rational action as paradigmatic, introducing affectual and other non-rational elements only when strictly necessary to account for deviations allows social scientists to analyse large areas of social life in these terms. So, at a rather different level do the normalizing discourses of psychiatry, penology, and the like (Foucault, 1977, 1979, Douzelot, 1979, Rose, 1985).

What is required then for talk of rational economic man and his relations to be implicated in significant areas of social life is that participants should not be confronted with too many apparent departures from the norm, and that there should be ways of explaining away whatever departures cannot be ignored. It must be possible, for example, to assimilate the decision-making processes in most capitalist enterprises, or at least their outcomes, more or less closely to the model of rational economic actor. Such requirements will, of course, be relaxed for the very young, the senile, and others judged to have departed considerably from the rational norm. For the rest, models of rational action are implicated in significant areas of social life to the extent that the relevant actors make use of such models in their own assessments and decisions. To say that, of course, is not to say that other significant elements might not also be involved, or that the models are descriptively adequate to the actors' own behaviour.

What of its theoretical claims, to parsimony and explanatory power? I have argued that there are two respects in which the claims to parsimony are more apparent than real. First, rational choice analysis employs a model of the actor involving specific refinements of the portfolio model, which is itself a considerable refinement of the most elementary model of the actor as locus of decision and action. We have seen that complex and highly questionable assumptions are built into the apparently simple model of maximizing behaviour. Secondly, many of the apparently powerful results of rational choice analyses depend on an implicit structural determination of the forms of thought employed by actors.

However, the more important point to notice here is that rational choice analysis has paid a very high price for its theoretical parsimony. We saw in chapter 2 how Olson claims to use a few abstract principles to generate explanatory theories that can be applied across a wide range of situations and societies. The trouble with explanations that do rely on distinctive features of the society in question is that they cannot be tested 'against a broad enough array of data or experience' (Olson, 1982, p.10). Explanation must abstract from all but the most essential features – supposing, of course, that we know what those features are. Another way of looking at that claim is to note that Olson's 'explanations' require little knowledge of the society or situation in question. Explanation, in other words, can proceed on the basis of ignorance. We have seen, for example, how abstract principles, a small amount of historical knowledge and a few caricatures suffice, in Olson's view, to generate an explanation of Britain's relative economic decline.

In fact, few adherents of the rational choice approach make quite such extravagant claims for the explanatory potential of their work. Nevertheless, there remains a sense in which their theoretical parsimony is bought at too high a price. Rational choice analysis deliberately abstracts from the techniques and forms of thought employed by actors in their deliberations. The lack of realism here is justified on the grounds either that the assumption of rationality is a necessary simplification or that it provides a paradigm for the analysis of human behaviour in general. In either case the effect is to foreclose a considerable field of possible investigation concerning the forms of thought employed by actors and the social conditions on which they depend. The price of this attempt at parsimony is to limit the field of intellectual inquiry.

But what of the powerful results of rational choice analysis, what of its explanatory successes? Consider, for example, Hardin's comment that the assumption of narrowly rational motivations 'helps us to understand why half of eligible Americans do not vote, but it does little to help us understand the other half'(Hardin, 1982, p.11). In the latter case the assumption of narrow rationality provides a benchmark for assessing the impact of other motivations. I have already indicated how that claim to paradigmatic status limits the field of inquiry. What concerns us here is the other part of Hardin's comment, concerning our understanding of why so many Americans do not vote. The 'explanation' tells us what narrowly rational actors would do in the situation of the large numbers of Americans who do not vote, but it tells us nothing about what motivates the non-voters themselves. It takes no account of the forms of thought they employ, of the manner in which the question of whether to vote or not arises, if it arises at all, or the considerations that are taken into account when it does.

I have argued then that the parsimony of rational choice analysis is bought at too high a theoretical price and that its claims to explanatory power are largely spurious. Models of rational action provide tools that are widely used in modern societies and rational choice analysis is little more than an elaboration of that usage. My final comment concerns the political implications of rational choice analyses. Here are Olson's comments on the implications of his arguments for macroeconomic policy. The most important implication

is that the best macroeconomic policy is a good micro-economic policy. There is no substitute for a more open and competitive environment. If combinations dominate markets throughout the economy and the government is always intervening on behalf of special interests, there is no macroeconomic policy that can put things right. (p.233)

Imagine a society in which the majority had been persuaded of the truth of these arguments. It might well adopt

the most obvious and far-reaching remedy: it might simply repeal all special-interest legislation or regulation and at the same time apply rigorous anti-trust laws to every type of cartel or collusion that used its power to obtain prices or wages above competitive levels. A society could in this way keep distributional coalitions from doing any substantial damage. (p.236)

Olson recognizes that such a development is unlikely, but the general direction of his policy prescriptions is clear. It is also clear that some special interests will be better placed than others to protect themselves against the prospects of hostile legislation, or against its effects if implemented. The impact of some of these special interests would therefore continue to be felt, albeit in modified forms. Olson's prescriptions, then, have obvious distributional implications, but there is no reason to expect them to remedy the condition for which they are prescribed.

Not all adherents of the rational choice approach would support Olson's policy prescriptions. In spite of the efforts of Olson and of the public choice theorists discussed in chapter 2, it would be a mistake to identify rational choice analysis with some version of the politics of the New Right. The real problem posed by the attempt to draw political conclusions from abstract analyses of the kind that Olson presents is rather different. Consider the view that what the consequences of legislation, or any other political action, are in a given situation must depend on the particular features of that situation. From that point of view prescription for political action would have to be based on careful investigation of the conditions in which the proposed action is to take place, including the techniques and forms of thought employed by the relevant actors. To proceed otherwise, on the basis of an account of what idealized rational actors would do and an analysis that deliberately abstracts from distinctive features of the situation, would then be irresponsible.

Notes

1   Introduction

1   We shall see in chapter 4 that it is sometimes used by those who favour a rather different conception of the actor's rationality. See references in chapter 4, note 6.
2   The most forceful statements of the merits of the rational choice approach are in Olson, 1965, 1982, and Becker, 1976. More measured accounts can be found in Hardin, 1982, and the introduction to Elster (ed.), 1986.
3   Elster brings out this feature of rational choice analysis very clearly. See Elster, 1979, 1983a.
4   See Hollis and Lukes, 1982, for a recent selection.
5   Rather different versions of the dualism of scheme and reality are used in Winch, 1970, Kuhn, 1970, and Feyerabend, 1975, 1978.

2   The rational choice approach to social behaviour

1   See the discussion in Toye, 1976.
2   There are excellent surveys in Barry and Hardin, 1982, and Sen, 1977b.
3   Closely related accounts of Britain's economic problems have been advanced by Goldthorpe, 1978, Beer, 1982, and many others. I have discussed some of these accounts in Hindess, 1986c.
4   See Mueller, 1979, for a general exposition, and the collections of Buchanan *et al.*, 1978, and Buchanan, 1986.
5   There are good examples of this line of argument in Friedman and Friedman, 1980, and Beer, 1982.
6   See Laver, 1981, for a non-technical discussion.
7   For examples see Lash and Urry, 1984, Carling, 1986, Roemer (ed.), 1986.
8   'Endowments' is a technical term derived from Roemer's (1982) reworking of the concept of exploitation in terms of game theory. Endowments may include property, skills, and 'more subtle cultural traits' (Elster, 1985, p. 330).

3   Rationality, egoism and social atomism

1   Weber's views on formal and substantive rationality are discussed in Brubaker, 1984.
2   Different versions of this view of individual rationality can be found in MacIntyre, 1981, Parfit, 1984, and Williams, 1985.

3 I owe this point to Philip Pettit. See, especially, Pettit, 1988.
4 In fact a variety of other positions has always been available, for
   example, in Elias's figurational sociology, Giddens's notion of the
   'duality of structure', and the ethnomethodological insistence that
   action occurs in settings. I have discussed the complicity between
   individualism and structuralism in Hindess, 1986a.
5 Taylor, 1982, is a good example.
6 Williams, Williams and Thomas, 1983, Tomlinson, 1982, Thompson, 1986.
7 Winter has used this strategy to great effect in his critique of
   the neo-classical theory of the firm (Winter, 1964, 1971, Nelson
   and Winter, 1982). A closely related strategy is employed by
   Hirschman in *Exit, Voice and Loyalty*.

4 Models of the actor

1 Dennett (1969), for example, treats the ascription of propositional
   attitudes as a useful explanatory device without any ontological weight. I argue below for a realist position on this point;
   propositional attitudes have an explanatory significance for action
   only if they play a part in the decisions of the relevant actors.
2 There are excellent discussions of Davidson's arguments in Hacking, 1975, and Macdonald and Pettit, 1981. The latter deal
   particularly with their implications for the social sciences.
3 For example, Ryle, 1949, Dray, 1957, Hampshire, 1959, and
   'most of the books in the series edited by R. F. Holland, Studies
   in Philosophical Psychology' (Davidson, 1980, p. 3). Winch, 1958,
   is perhaps the most familiar of these books to social scientists.
4 See 'Mental Events' and 'Psychology as philosophy', both in
   Davidson, 1980.
5 Hirst and Woolley, 1982, Hollis and Lukes, 1982, Macdonald
   and Pettit, 1981, Doyal and Harris, 1986.
6 The principle of humanity is proposed as an alternative to Davidson's principle of charity by Grandy, 1973. The differences are
   discussed in Macdonald and Pettit, 1981, chapter 1, and in Lukes's
   contribution to Hollis and Lukes, 1982.
7 See Hollis, 1979b (and Horton's reply, 1979) and Hollis's contribution to Hollis and Lukes, 1982.
8 Compare the discussion of this issue in Hirst and Woolley,
   1982.
9 See Thompson, 1986, for further discussion of the implications
   of this point.

5 Rationality, action and deliberation

1 If intention is understood strictly as a matter of propositional
   attitudes then only creatures with language can be said to form

intentions. See essay 11 in Davidson, 1984. For more general
discussion of the differences and similarities between human
and animal thought see Hirst and Woolley, 1982, part 1, and
Walker, 1983.

2 Many of his most influential papers are collected in Simon, 1979,
1982. See also March's contribution to Elster (ed.), 1986.

3 The point is forcefully made in the introduction to Elster (ed.),
1986.

4 Foucault, 1967, 1970, 1972, 1973, 1977. See the discussion of
these works in Cousins and Hussain, 1984.

5 I have discussed some of these early Marxist debates in Hindess,
1983.

6 Becker, 1976, Friedman, 1953. A similar case is often argued
in Marxist discussions of the corporation, for example, in Baran
and Sweezy, 1968.

7 For recent discussions see Brubaker, 1984, and the contributions
to Lash and Whimster, 1987.

8 The taken-for-granted character of our specialized techniques
for relating to the natural world is a theme of many of Husserl's
later writings. See especially Husserl, 1970, and the discussion in
Derrida, 1978.

6 Individualism and social structure

1 For recent examples see Knorr-Cetina and Cicourel, 1981, Giddens, 1984, Hindess, 1986a.

2 See Cutler *et al.*, 1977–8, Vol II, and the discussion of Althusser's
account of the subject in Hirst, 1979.

3 Feuerstein and others have argued that it is often possible considerably to increase the IQs of children regarded as backward
by means of appropriate training. See the discussion of the
educational implications of this view in Sharron, 1987.

4 cf. Foucault's polemics against this view of power in his 1977,
1979, 1980.

5 Weber takes what he regards as distinctive features of the human
individual as the essence of the actor. A diametrically opposed
essentialism can be found in Coleman's argument (1974, 1982)
that there are two kinds of person: natural and corporate. In
his view the importance of corporate actors in the modern world
indicates the emergence of a fundamentally new kind of society
characterized by what he calls asymmetric relationships between
natural persons and corporations. I discuss Coleman's arguments
in Hindess, 1989.

6 See Thompson, 1986, especially chapter 7.

7 See the discussion in Tomlinson, 1982. A different example can
be found in the Friedmans' (1980) account of the corporation as
a mere intermediary for its stockholders.

8 This is the standard Marxist account, but there are more sophisticated versions. See, for example, many of the essays in Goldthorpe (ed.), 1984, and see Clegg *et al.*, 1986.

References

Arrow, K. (1963) *Individual Values and Social Choice* (New York: Wiley).

Baran, P. A. and Sweezy, P. (1968), *Monopoly Capitalism* (New York: Monthly Review Press).

Barry B. (1978), *Sociologists, Economists and Democracy*, 2nd edn (Chicago: University of Chicago Press).

Barry, B. and Hardin, R. (eds) (1982), *Rational Man and Irrational Society* (Beverly Hills, Calif. and London: Sage).

Becker, G. S. (1976), *The Economic Approach to Human Behaviour* (Chicago: University of Chicago Press).

Beer, S. (1982), *Britain Against Itself: the political contradictions of collectivism* (London: Faber).

Brittan, S. (1978), 'Inflation and democracy', in F. Hirsch and J. H. Goldthorpe (eds) (1978), *The Political Economy of Inflation* (Oxford: Martin Robertson), pp. 161-85.

Brubaker, R. (1984), *The Limits of Rationality* (London: Allen & Unwin).

Buchanan, J. M. (1986), *Liberty, Market and State* (Brighton: Wheatsheaf).

Buchanan, J. M. and Wagner, R.E. (1977), *Democracy in Deficit*, (London: Academic Press).

Buchanan, J. M. *et al.* (1978), *The Economics of Politics* (London, Institute of Economic Affairs).

Cairncross, A. (1985), *Years of Recovery: British Economic Policy*, 1945–51 (London: Methuen).

Carling, A. (1986), 'Rational choice Marxism', *New Left Review*, 161.

Clegg, S., Boreham, P., and Dow, G. (1986), *Class, Politics and the Economy* (London: Routledge & Kegan Paul).

Coleman, J. S. (1974), *Power and the Structure of Society* (New York: Norton).

Coleman, J. S. (1982), *The Assymetric Society* (Syracuse: Syracuse University Press).

Cousins, M. and Hussain, A. (1984), *Michel Foucault* (London: Macmillan).

Cutler, A. J., Hindess, B., Hirst, P. Q., and Hussain, A. (1977–8) *Marx's Capital and Capitalism Today*, two vols (London: Routledge & Kegan Paul).

Davidson, D. (1980), *Essays on Actions and Events* (Oxford: Clarendon Press).

Davidson, D. (1984), *Inquiries into Truth and Interpretation* (Oxford: Clarendon Press).

Dennett, D. C. (1969), *Content and Consciousness* (London: Routledge and Kegan Paul).
Derrida, J. (1978), *Edmund Husserl's: The Origins of Geometry* (Brighton: Harvester).
Donzelot, J. (1979), *The Policing of Families* (New York: Pantheon).
Downs, A. (1957), *An Economic Theory of Democracy* (New York: Harper).
Doyal, L. and Harris, R. (1986), *Empiricism, Explanation and Rationality* (London: Routledge & Kegan Paul).
Dray, W. (1957), *Laws and Explanation in History* (Oxford: Clarendon Press).
Elster, J. (1978), *Logic and Society* (Chichester and New York: Wiley).
Elster, J. (1979), *Ulysses and the Sirens* (Cambridge: Cambridge University Press).
Elster, J. (1983a), *Explaining Technical Change* (Cambridge: Cambridge University Press).
Elster, J. (1983b), *Sour Grapes* (Cambridge: Cambridge University Press).
Elster, J. (1985), *Making Sense of Marx* (Cambridge: Cambridge University Press).
Elster, J. (ed.) (1986), *Rational Choice* (Oxford: Blackwell).
Evans-Pritchard, E. E. (1976), *Witchcraft, Oracles and Magic Among the Azande*, abridged edn (Oxford: Clarendon Press).
Feyerabend, P. (1975), *Against Method* (London: New Left Books).
Feyerabend, P. (1978), *Science in a Free Society* (London: New Left Books).
Foucault, M. (1967), *Madness and Civilization* (London: Tavistock).
Foucault, M. (1970), *The Order of Things* (London: Tavistock).
Foucault, M. (1972), *The Archeology of Knowledge* (London: Tavistock).
Foucault, M. (1973), *The Birth of the Clinic* (London: Tavistock).
Foucault, M. (1977), *Discipline and Punish* (London: Allen Lane).
Foucault, M. (1979), *The History of Secularity (Vol I)* (London: Allen Lane).
Foucault, M. (1980), *Power/Knowledge* (Brighton: Harvester).
Friedman, M. (1953), 'The methodology of positive economics', in *Essays in Positive Economics* (Chicago: University of Chicago Press).
Friedman, M. and Friedman, R. (1980), *Free to Choose* (Harmondsworth: Penguin).
Giddens, A. (1984), *The Constitution of Society* (Oxford: Polity).
Goldthorpe, J. H. (1978), 'The current inflation: towards a sociological account', in F. Hirsch and J. H. Goldthorpe (eds) (1978), *The Political Economy of Inflation* (Oxford: Martin Robertson), pp. 186–213.

Goldthorpe, J. H. (ed.) (1984), *Order and Conflict in Contemporary Capitalism* (Oxford: Clarendon Press).
Grandy, R. (1973), 'Reference, meaning and belief', *Journal of Philosophy*, 70, pp. 439–52.
Hacking, I. (1975), *Why Does Language Matter to Philosophy?* (Cambridge: Cambridge University Press).
Hacking, I. (1982), 'Language, Truth and Reason', in M. Hollis and S. Lukes (eds), *Rationality and Relativism* (Oxford: Blackwell), pp. 48–66.
Hahn, F. and Hollis, M. (1979), *Philosophy and Economic Theory* (Oxford: Oxford University Press).
Hampshire, S. (1959), *Thought and Action* (London: Chatto and Windus).
Hardin, R. (1982), *Collective Action* (Baltimore, Md: Johns Hopkins University Press).
Hindess, B. (1983), *Parliamentary Democracy and Socialist Politics*, (London: Routledge & Kegan Paul).
Hindess, B. (1984), 'Rational choice theory and the analysis of political action', *Economy and Society*, 13, pp. 255–77.
Hindess, B. (1986a), 'Actors and social relations', in S. Turner and M. Wardell (eds), *Sociological Theory in Transition* (London: Allen & Unwin), pp. 113–126.
Hindess, B. (1986b), 'Interests in political analysis', in J. Law (ed.), *Power, Action and Belief*, Sociological Review Monograph 32 (London: Routledge & Kegan Paul), pp. 112–131.
Hindess, B. (1986c), *Freedom, Equality and the Market* (London: Tavistock).
Hindess, B. (1987a), *Politics and Class Analysis* (Oxford: Blackwell).
Hindess, B. (1987b), 'Rationalization and the characterization of modern society', in S. Lash and S. Whimster (eds), *Max Weber: studies in rationality and irrationality* (London: Allen & Unwin), pp. 137-53.
Hindess, B. (1988), 'Class analysis as social theory', in P. Lassmann (ed.) *Politics and Social Theory* (London: British Sociological Association).
Hindess, B. (1989), *Political Choice and Social Structure* (London: Edward Elgar).
Hirsch, F. and Goldthorpe, J. H. (eds), (1978), *The Political Economy of Inflation* (Oxford: Martin Robertson).
Hirschman, A. (1970), *Exit, Voice and Loyalty* (Cambridge, Mass.: Harvard University Press).
Hirschman, A. (1982), *Shifting Involvements: private interest and public action* (Oxford: Martin Robertson).
Hirst, P. Q. (1979), *On Law and Ideology* (London: Macmillan).
Hirst, P. Q. and Woolley, P. (1982), *Social Relations and Human Attributes* (London: Tavistock).

126   *Choice, Rationality, and Social Theory*

Hollis, M. and Lukes, S. (eds) (1982), *Rationality and Relativism* (Oxford: Blackwell).
Hollis, M. (1979a), 'Rational man and social science', in R. Harrison (ed.), *Rational Action* (Cambridge: Cambridge University Press) pp. 1-16.
Hollis, M. (1979b), 'The epistemological unity of mankind', in S. C. Brown (ed.), *Philosophical Disputes in the Social Sciences* (Brighton: Harvester).
Hollis, M. (1981), 'Economic man and original sin', *Political Studies*, 29, pp. 167–180.
Hollis, M. (1983), 'Rational preferences', *The Philosophical Forum*, 14, pp. 246–262.
Horton, R. (1979), 'Reply to Martin Hollis', in S. C. Brown (ed.), *Philosophical Disputes in the Social Sciences* (Brighton: Harvester).
Husserl, E. (1970), *The Crisis of European Sciences and Transcendental Phenomenology* (Evanston, Ill.: Northwestern University Press).
Keynes, M. (1936), *The General Theory of Employment, Interest and Money* (London: Macmillan).
Knorr-Cetina, K. and Cicourel, A. (eds) (1981), *Advances in Social Theory and Methodology: towards an integration of micro- and macro-sociology* (London: Routledge & Kegan Paul).
Kuhn, T. (1970), *The Structure of Scientific Revolutions* (Chicago: Chicago University Press).
Lash, S. and Urry, J. (1984), 'The new Marxism of collective action', *Sociology*, 18, pp. 33–50.
Lash, S. and Whimster, S. (ed.) (1987), *Max Weber, Rationality and Modernity* (London: Allen and Unwin).
Laver, M. (1981), *The Politics of Private Desires* (Harmondsworth: Penguin).
McDonald, D. G. (1969), *Union Man* (New York: Dutton).
Macdonald, G. and Pettit, P. (1981), *Semantics and Social Science* (London: Routledge & Kegan Paul).
MacIntyre, A. (1981), *After Virtue* (London: Duckworth).
March, J. G. (1986), 'Bounded rationality, ambiguity, and the engineering of choice', in J. Elster (ed.) (1986), *Rational Choice* (Oxford: Blackwell), pp. 142–170.
Marx, K. and Engels, F. (1970), preface (1872) to 'The communist manifesto', in *Collected Works* (London: Lawrence and Wishart).
Mauss, M. (1979), 'Body techniques', in *Sociology and Psychology* (London: Routledge and Kegan Paul).
Mueller, D. (1979), *Public Choice* (Cambridge: Cambridge University Press).
Nelson, R. and Winter, S. G. (1982), *An Evolutionary Theory of Economic Change* (Cambridge, Mass.: Harvard University Press).
Olson, M. (1965), *The Logic of Collective Action* (Cambridge, Mass.:

Harvard University Press).

Olson, M. (1982), *The Rise and Decline of Nations* (New Haven: Yale University Press).

Parfit, D. (1984), *Reasons and Persons* (Oxford: Oxford University Press).

Parsons, T. and Shils, E. (1962), *Towards a General Theory of Action* (New York: Harper).

Pettit, P. (1988), 'Social holism without collectivism', in E. Margalit (ed.), *Israeli Colloquium in History and Philosophy of Science*, Vol. 4 (Dordrecht: Reidel).

Przeworski, A. (1985), *Capitalism and Social Democracy* (Cambridge: Cambridge University Press).

Przeworski, A. and Sprague, J. (1986), *Paper Stones* (Chicago: Chicago University Press).

Quine, W. V. O. (1960), *Word and Object* (New York: Wiley).

Rawls, J. (1972), *A Theory of Justice* (Oxford: Oxford University Press).

Riker, W. (1962), *The Theory of Political Coalitions* (New Haven Conn.: Yale University Press).

Riker, W. and Ordershook, P. C. (1973), *An Introduction to Positive Political Theory* (Englewood Cliffs, N.J.: Prentice-Hall).

Roemer, J. (1982), *A General Theory of Exploitation and Class* (Cambridge, Mass.: Harvard University Press).

Roemer, J. (ed.) (1986), *Analytical Marxism* (Cambridge University Press).

Rose, N. (1985), *The Psychological Complex: social relations and the psychology of the individual* (London: Methuen).

Ryle, G. (1949), *The Concept of Mind* (London: Hutchinson).

Schick, F. (1984), *Having Reasons: an essay on rationality and sociality* (Princeton, NJ: Princeton University Press).

Sen, A. (1977a), 'Rational fools: a critique of the behavioural foundations of economic theory', *Philosophy and Public Affairs*, 6, pp. 317–344.

Sen, A. (1977b), 'Social choice theory: a re-examination', *Econometrica*, 45, pp. 53–89.

Sen, A. (1981), *Poverty and Famines: an essay on entitlement and deprivation* (Oxford: Clarendon Press).

Sen, A. (1983), *Choice, Welfare and Measurement* (Oxford: Blackwell).

Sharron, H. (1987), *Changing Children's Minds* (London: Souvenir Press).

Simon, H. A. (1979), *Models of Thought* (New Haven, Conn: Yale University Press).

Simon, H.A. (1982), *Models of Bounded Rationality* (Cambridge, Mass.: MIT Press).

Taylor, M. (1982), *Community, Anarchy and Liberty* (Cambridge:

Cambridge University Press).
Thompson, G. (1986), *Economic Calculation and Policy Formation* (London: Routledge & Kegan Paul).
Tomlinson, J. (1981), 'The "economics of public expenditure" *Economy and Society*, 10, pp. 389–402.
Tomlinson, J. (1982), *The Unequal Struggle: British socialism and the capitalist enterprise* (London: Methuen).
Toye, J. (1976), 'Economic theories of politics and public finance', *British Journal of Political Science*, 6, pp. 433–447.
Walker, S. (1983), *Animal Thought* (London: Routledge & Kegan Paul).
Williams, B. (1979), 'Internal and external reasons', in R. Harrison (ed.), *Rational Action* (Cambridge University Press), pp. 17–28.
Williams, B. (1985), *Ethics and the Limits of Philosophy* (London: Fontana).
Williams, J., Williams, K. and Thomas, D. (1983), *Why Are the British Bad at Manufacturing?* (London: Routledge & Kegan Paul).
Williams, K. and Haslam, C. (1986), 'Accounting for failure', *Economy and Society*, 15.
Winch, P. (1958), *The Idea of a Social Science and its Relation to Philosophy* (London: Routledge & Kegan Paul).
Winch, P. (1970), 'Understanding a primitive society', in B. R. Wilson (ed.), *Rationality* (Oxford: Blackwell), pp. 78–111.
Winter, S. G. (1964), 'Economic natural selection and the theory of the firm', *Yale Economic Essays*, 4, pp. 225–272.
Winter, S. G. (1971), 'Satisficing, selection and the innovating remnant', *Quarterly Journal of Economics*, 85, pp. 237–261.

Index

actors, *see* models of actors
akrasia, *see* incontinence
Arrow, K.: on individual preferences and collective decisions 11-12

Barry, B. 3
Becker, Gary: on rational choice analysis 1-2
Britain
coal crisis, 1946-7 63-4
theory on progress stultified by special-interest organizations 17
British Steel 84
Brittan, S. 20
Buchanan, J.M. *et al.*
Economics of Politics, The 19
on public expenditure 19-20
Buchanan, J.M. and Wagner, R.E. 20
polemic against Keynes 21

capitalist enterprises
competition 83
deliberation 84
irrationality 25, 107
modes of calculation 83-4
profit maximization 83, 84
Center for the Study of Public Choice, Virginia 19
China: guild-ridden stagnation 17
choice 1
rational 30, 31
Cutler, A. *et al.* 84

Davidson, Donald 7, 53, 58, 68, 69, 89

'Actions, reasons and causes' 50
critique of dualism of scheme and reality 72, 75-7, 79
investigation of intentional explanation 49
on actions in 'the right way' 51
'On the very idea of a conceptual scheme' 75
principle of charity 6, 57, 58, 62, 63, 76, 77, 80, 81, 88, 101
disasters due to ways of thinking 63-5
Douzelot, J. 114
Downs, A. 22
assumption of rationality 11
Economic Theory of Democracy, An 9, 18
on individuals as utility maximizers 9-10, 19
on government decision-making as maximization of votes 18-19
on politicians and voters as rational and self-serving agents 19, 70
on public expenditure 19-20
on testing models by accuracy of predictions 10

egoism 29, 33-5, 42-3
fitting egoism into rational choice approach 33
Elster, Jon 3, 22, 49, 52, 94
definition of class 25
definition of rationality 25, 26
Making Sense of Marx 23
on capitalists' irrationality 25, 107
on confusion of class interests with society's 23, 24

129

Elster, Jon *cont.*
on intentional explanation 48-9
on methodological collectivism 36,
37, 94, 95, 106
on opportunities and behaviour 38
on optimizing behaviour paradigm
2, 33
on unintended consequences 25, 106
Rational Choice 48
reconstruction of Marx's social
theory 22, 23-5, 93, 95, 105, 106
Evans-Pritchard, E.E. 90
behaviour during fieldwork 90-1
*Witchcraft, Oracles and Magic
among the Azande* 58, 71, 88, 90

Feyerabend, P. 73
on scientific thought 71, 74
Foucault, M. 71, 91, 114
Friedman, M.: on unrealistic
assumptions yielding realistic
predictions 10

Giddens, A.
Constitution of Society, The 100
on 'knowledgeable' agents 100, 101
partial definition of 'action' 45

Hacking, I. 58
'styles of reasoning' concept 71-3,
77-83 *passim*, 87
Hahn, F and Hollis, M. 30
Hardin, R. 3
on extra-rational considerations in
collective action 35
on narrowly rational assumptions
yielding useful predictions
10-11, 33, 35, 61, 62-3, 116
Hindess, B. 102, 110, 113
Hirschman, A. 31, 32
Hirst, P. and Woolley, P. 113
Hollis, M. 30, 37, 41
assumptions in rational choice
approach 29
on actor's real interest 36
on social atomism 35, 36

I Ching 88, 89, 98
incontinence (weakness of will) 51-2
physiological processes 52, 54
individualism and social structure
7-8, 93

methodological individualism 25,
27, 36, 93-7, 103

Keynes, J.M. 21
General Theory 21, 91
on economists' influence 21-2, 91
Kuhn, T. 73
on scientific thought 71, 74

Laplace, Pierre-Simon 72-3
Lash, S. and Urry, J. 22
leadership training 85

McDonald, D.G.: on dues picketing
13
Macdonald, G. and Pettit, P. 31, 42,
46, 58, 61
on attitudinal rationality 54-5, 66
on beliefs and desires as
propositional attitudes 47
on portfolio model 50
Margolis 34
Marx, Karl 22, 23, 25, 93
Capital 23
on lessons of Paris Commune (with
Engels) 81-2
Mauss, M.: example of specificity of
techniques 85-6
methodological collectivism 36, 37,
93-4, 95, 106
models of actors 5, 42-4
action consequent upon belief and
desire 86, 89, 92
actors' deliberations 79, 84, 85, 87,
88, 89, 91, 96, 102, 105-9, 110,
112
actors' specialized techniques
86-91 *passim*, 96, 99, 108, 109,
111
actors' tools 97-8
attitudinal rationality 50, 54-60,
66, 67
behavioural rationality 30, 33, 42,
46, 57, 50-4, 66
forms of decisions 47-8
forms of thought and social
locations 110-11, 112
'knowledgeable' agents 100-2
minimal concept of actor 44-8
portfolio model 5, 6, 39, 44, 45,
48-50, 55, 59, 60, 61, 66-7, 68,
79, 80, 90, 98, 99, 108, 109

rational choice model 44, 113
rational preference structure 42
rationality by actor's category 43,
    107-8
social actors 5, 46-7, 49, 54, 67-8,
    84, 102-5

National Coal Board 84
Nelson, R. and Winter, S.G. 83

Oedipus 51
Olson, Mancur 13, 21, 115
  aims 15
  Logic of Collective Action, The 15
  on accumulation of special-interest
    organizations in stable societies
    17
  on ineffectiveness of special-
    interest organizations 16
  on irrelevance of individual
    sacrifice 14-15
  on macroeconomic policy 116-17
  on rational individuals and
    collective action 16, 95, 105
  on stultification caused by special-
    interest organizations 17-18, 19
  Rise and Decline of Nations, The 4,
    13, 15-18

Parsons, Talcott
  and Shils, E. 53
  on forces behind human actions 53
  *Towards a General Theory of
    Action* 53
political analysis 81-3
  economics of politics 18-22
  Marxist socialism 88
  See also Downs, A. and
    Przeworski, A.
Prisoner's Dilemma 12, 33
  difficulty of securing collective
    interest 12-13
Public Choice 19
Przeworski, A. 39
  concept of methodological
    individualism 25, 27
  on importance of actors' choices
    27, 28
  view of social structure 37-8
  work on development of social
    democratic politics 22, 25-8, 63

Przeworski, A. and Sprague, J.: on
    class 26, 27

Quine, W.V.O. 71
  on indeterminacy of translation
    74-5, 79

rational choice analyses 1-4, 7-8, 66, 93
  assumption of actor's rationality 3,
    106
  modification of portfolio model 61
  optimizing behaviour paradigm 3-4
  scope of present book 2-8
rational choice approach to social
    behaviour 4, 9
  application of rational self-
    interested model 9-10
  assumptions regarding actors 29-30
  economics of politics 18-22
  egoism, *see* separate entry
  free-rider problem 14
  generation of widely applicable
    theories 18
  individual incentives needed 13-14
  individual sacrifice irrelevant 14-15
  lack of realism as simplification or
    accepted as human 11
  motivations other than self-interest
    34, 35
  narrow rationality equated with
    self-interest 11
  new Marxism of collective action
    22-8, 36-7
  Prisoner's Dilemma 12-13, 33
  public choice theory 19, 22, 117
  self-interest opposed to collective
    interest 12, 13, 14
  social atomism, *see* separate entry
  'structural' constraints on
    individuals' choices 39-40
  See also Buchanan, J.M. and
    Olson, Mancur
rational economic man concept
    112-118
  accounting for failure 114
  question re explanatory power 115,
    116
  theoretical claims to parsimony
    115-16
rationality 1, 6, 30-3
  actions, reasons and causes 50-1,
    52